UNDAUNTED ASPIRATION

Lessons of Curiosity, Courage, Authenticity, and Purposeful Intention

KIM JENKINS

UNDAUNTED ASPIRATION
LESSONS OF CURIOSITY, COURAGE, AUTHENTICITY, AND PURPOSEFUL INTENTION

iUniverse books may be ordered through booksellers or by contacting:

iUniverse
1663 Liberty Drive
Bloomington, IN 47403
www.iuniverse.com
844-349-9409

ISBN: 978-1-6632-2799-7 (sc)
ISBN: 978-1-6632-2801-7 (hc)
ISBN: 978-1-6632-2800-0 (e)

Library of Congress Control Number: 2021917222

Print information available on the last page.

iUniverse rev. date: 02/11/2022

Thank You

As the idea of writing a book became a reality, I reflected on the people who were there in the moments that mattered. To each of you, I want to say "THANK YOU".

There were many people who cared enough to be my genuine sponsors, advocates, and coaches long before the terms became corporate buzz words. As I reflect on their authentic acts of caring and kindness, there are a few who deserve to be mentioned due to their contributions to my career path – and more important- due to their significant impact on my life journey.

- My Inroads crew – Miguel C, Ms. Gee, Tammi N.H.- they were willing to take chances to make a lump of carbon shine like a diamond.
- Chris M, Nancy M and Greg S – you all took a chance on a kid from the hood. You created opportunities, broke down barriers and were willing to teach me all the things I needed to

know. Your commitment to bridging the gaps and closing the loops helped make me a true contender in the game of life.

- John G – when I was ready to turn a corner, you paved the way.
- Neil C, George C, Kristin J and Bob Q – you saw a version of me that I never knew existed. You challenged me, you pushed the limits of what was capable, you opened doors for me and you advocated for me in places, and in moments, that mattered.
- Amy B, Shelby D.B, Don K – thanks for all the opportunities, for the support and advocacy and most importantly – for all the love and laughs.

To my *framily* - the friends in my life who have become a family – you are exactly what I need to keep me grounded, humble and whole at all times. I love you more than words can express.

And finally, to the little people who gave me so much joy during some of the toughest times in my life, who have grown up so quickly and have little people of their own who give me reasons to smile – Quiana and DuShane and their little ones DeAndre and Dior – Auntie loves you with all her heart and soul. We have been through a lot together, and life has not been fair, but we are still enjoying this game called life in the best ways we can.

I would not be who I am without the care, concern and love I received from all of the individuals mentioned here. For that, I wanted to pause and make sure to say THANK YOU!

I am appreciative, grateful and blessed,
Kim

Contents

PART III—PURPOSE, PASSION, LEGACY

Preface

Someone once said, "People see your glory, but they don't know your story." I am always reminded of that when I speak to people about my life. They see who I am today and where I am today. I wouldn't refer to anything about my life as having *glory*. It's just my life. Each of our lives are built on the foundation of our experiences, our exposures, our desires, our dreams, our values, our efforts, our willingness, and our sacrifices. My life is also built upon my curiosity, the insatiable desire that fuels my thoughts and dreams and always makes me wonder, *What if*…

My life—my story—is about rising above barriers to find my version of success. It is about the journey that life is and how you can unlock your potential to reach any finish line you set your mind on, regardless of the obstacles you have to overcome. We are all on this voyage together, living our lives and searching for our purpose. Your dreams may seem out of reach to some, but you have the power to dare to dream beyond your imagination and realize your true potential. I believe we all have the ability to design our path and pave our road along our journey of life.

Introduction—Let's Talk

I am often asked to speak at conferences, make a presentation in a learning session, or participate in a panel discussion. In addition, I am also called upon to serve as an executive coach for individuals who are looking for guidance in their careers. These things happen because of the titles connected to my name—BA, CPA, CFO, CDIO, director, executive and so on. The roles I have held during my career draw people and provide strangers with some sense of understanding of my capabilities and experiences. As an introvert, I am not always excited about the possibility of public speaking. As someone who doesn't impress herself, I often wonder, *What do I have to say that anyone wants to hear?* I am often reminded that my story, while not unique, is inspiring to some. For that reason, I always agree to help when asked.

I am an open book, always willing to share my truth—unfiltered, unashamed, and comfortable with my path. Perhaps I am not always confident, but my truth is my truth, and I find value in everything I have been through.

One day, I found myself sitting with one of my protégés, enjoying lunch in one of my favorite quiet places, having a conversation about my career choices. I like being outside on a warm, sunny day. Something about the sunlight, and the colors of the spaces around us, makes me smile. I enjoy watching the universe do what it does—trees growing, flowers blooming, the sky hovering above us, the air blowing softly, people moving along and going about their days. We are just two people in this massive, amazing system of life, enjoying a peaceful moment talking, sharing, learning, and growing.

My life is a series of choices. It is methodical and strategic. The things I can control, I try to manage. The things I can't control, I try to influence. Things beyond my control and my influence pique my curiosity. My protégé is focused, committed, and ambitious, and I thoroughly enjoy our time together. While I am mentoring, I, too, am learning. There is reciprocal value in this experience, and I enjoy sharing my story in the hope that it can help someone who may be experiencing the things I have lived thorough. If my story touches one person and encourages them to dream, I will have served my purpose.

Today, the question from my protégé was loaded, and I decided to be vulnerable and share my entire story. So here we go …

PART I

CHILDHOOD REALITIES

Chapter 1

INSECURITIES

I CAN STILL HEAR MY MOTHER SAYING THE WORDS today: "You better be smart, 'cause you aren't as pretty as she is." Her words rang in my ears and left an indelible mark on me that I still can't shake. This was the underling source of all of my insecurities. It was the catalyst for my desire to find a way to seek the best education available to me—to be *smart*, as I had been advised. This was a consistent theme that followed me, and it always made me feel like I was never enough—like I was less than and not worthy. The way she treated me made it easy for others to treat me the same way. I never understood it, and as a child, I tried really hard to figure out what I was doing wrong. I finally settled into the inferior space that had been created for me. I wasn't as pretty as she was. There was nothing I could do about that, so I had to learn to be OK with it. I had to act like the stares and looks and gestures - from extended family members and neighbors - didn't bother me. I had to act like I didn't recognize the comparisons that were consistently being made between us. I had to learn to smile through it all. As a child, that was a lot to manage, and it hurt. But I had been given a directive. I was advised to be smart, and that would be my complete focus.

As I think of those memories, the feelings begin to surface as they always did back then, and then a comfort comes over me. My mind transitions to my safe space, and I recall a happy moment when I could hear the deafening roar of an airplane soaring above my head. As my thoughts take me to that place, I am transported into a moment at the airport, and I recall the experience …

The loud whirring sounds faded into the distance as the aircraft became a few flickering lights in the nighttime sky. Another airplane was beginning to take off in the distance. I knew because I heard what sounded like a giant kettle whistling, followed by the unbridled romance of the nighttime sky and its tumultuous, rumbling visitor. A few minutes later, silence shrouded the night.

"The Continental Airlines plane is probably going

to a warm, sunny location, with beach resorts where families spend their vacation time. The TWA plane could be going to a conference resort where professionals conduct their meetings while enjoying a round of golf. Where do you think the other one is headed, Daddy?"

Daddy ran a wrinkled hand through his graying hair before saying, "Hmmm, it could be going anywhere in the world. I could tell you what I think, but I'm more interested in knowing where your imagination will take it, Kimmy."

Daddy was my safe space. He didn't allow me to wallow in my insecurities or think I was less than anything. He encouraged me to think without limits. He always helped me silence my mind and my thoughts whenever he sensed something made me feel bad. He realized Mom had her favorite, and he overcompensated to make sure I felt favored as well. This balancing act was critical during my upbringing, though I didn't realize how significant it was at the time.

Chapter 2

HERITAGE

I THOUGHT ABOUT SOME OF MY FONDEST MEMORIES of my childhood as I sipped on tea and narrated my experiences to the protégé I had taken under my wing. The aspiring individual wanted to know more about my journey and how my desire to dream of a life beyond my existing environment had created the light along my path. I proceeded to tell her that growing up in the inner city of Newark, New Jersey, my world had merely consisted of a couple of neighboring cities. All I really knew was my neighborhood; apart from sporadic summer road trips we made to visit our paternal extended family down south, that was the scope of the universe for me. I enjoyed those trips to North Carolina because my paternal grandmother, Grandma Daisy, was a wealth of knowledge. She shared stories about growing up without her mother, who had passed away during childbirth.

When I asked Grandma Daisy about her blue eyes, she told me her father had blue eyes. Her father, my paternal great-grandfather, was the man who owned her family. He had a relationship with her mother, his servant. The reality of that sank in for my protégé. My great-grandmother was a servant, a slave who was owned by a family. My life, my story, becomes more meaningful to me as I reflect on what this means. The journey my ancestors made to overcome the realities of their existence, where they were viewed as property with no human rights, to create a path where I could choose the life I wanted to live—this is what consistently drives me.

Grandma Daisy and I would sit on her porch in North Carolina and rock in her chairs until she fell asleep talking. There were so many chairs and planters on the little porch; I always wondered how the adults could comfortably maneuver their way to a seat. There was a lot of love and laughter on that porch—and all of the sweet tea and red Kool-Aid we could drink. Grandma Daisy's house always felt like love and sunshine. It felt safe and free of judgment. Most times. There was the occasional family drama that occurred during family get-togethers. Overall, though, Grandma Daisy's house felt like a safe space for me.

This was in stark contrast to the visits to my maternal grandmother's house in New Jersey. She treated us like we were a nuisance. I felt like a stranger in her house. She showed no affection toward me, no love—nothing I expected of a grandmother. However, she was a bundle of love when it came to my cousins. I never understood why, and I stopped trying. I don't know when I stopped trying to understand. One day, I just stopped caring, and that made all the difference in how I felt when I was forced to be there. But with Grandma Daisy, it was different. I couldn't wait to get to her house to feel the warm embrace of love that surrounded her home. The differences were distinct, and the variation permeated both sides of the family. One side felt welcoming and loving. The other felt judgmental and injurious.

Many of our family members migrated to the North to begin a better life rather than remaining in the southern states postslavery. As I think about it now, I can only imagine that anything would be a better option than the remnants of a slave society. While the actual practices may have been abolished, the reverberations of its repercussions kept impacting the psyche of, and opportunities for, subsequent generations in the South.

Even today in the United States, we are still impacted by the rules that governed slavery in this country. When I imagine what life must have been like, being denied the fundamental freedoms of existence, I am amazed to know some of my ancestors survived such a life.

My father migrated from North Carolina to build a new life for himself once he reached his teenage maturity. Actually, the family story states that he left before he was old enough, fueled by an unparalleled determination to create a successful life for himself. Everyone who knew him either believed he would make it work or absolutely knew better than to try to stop him. After all, he could always return home if he needed to. Daddy was a leader, and there was no doubt he was going to give it all he had to offer. He would never allow himself to stop seeking the success he dreamed of. Daddy was courageous.

My mother migrated from South Carolina to accompany her older siblings, who had already moved to New York and New Jersey. Mommy was a follower; she wasn't one to make noise or create a path for herself. She was more comfortable letting others lead and then safely following along. I can see how she and my father came together to be a couple. Daddy was comfortable when he was in control. Mommy was comfortable when someone else was in control. That made for a perfect match. One led, and one followed, and that was how it worked in our family when I was younger.

Daddy and Mommy both worked hard, but there was a difference in how they worked. Their personalities were opposites. Daddy filled a room the moment he walked in. Mommy didn't like attention. She didn't desire to be seen or heard; she preferred being home on the couch rather than out and about. Their relationship was one of a true extrovert and a true introvert peacefully coexisting to partner and raise a family.

Chapter 3

CURIOSITY: THINKING BEYOND BOUNDARIES

It concerned me when I saw people around me resigning to a confined life within the boxed-in constraints of the inner city. That was all we knew—and all most people around me wanted to know—but as I grew older, I realized that I did not want to resign myself to a kind of life simply because it was better than what those before me and around me had experienced. Somehow, I came to believe that if we have the freedom to pursue an array of opportunities, it would be a disservice to ourselves not to tap into the potential we possess. I wanted the opportunity to expand my horizons, and that is probably how my curiosity began.

Upon reflection, I can safely say I had a very happy childhood, and I always thought I had everything that I could want. But as I grew older, my dreams grew bigger than my experiences in my family and in our neighborhood. As I sought guidance from people around me, I realized most adults I came into contact with had never expanded their goals beyond what I refer to now as the defined scope. I have always been a go-getter, and it did not sit well with me to settle for what life gave me. Not only did I want to know all the possibilities life had to offer, I also wanted to know what I could offer life, and that was a question I did not see anyone around me asking.

This is not to say I was ever trying to break away from where I come from. That will forever be a part of my home and the foundation of everything I am today. I will always cherish the neighborhood I grew up in and how close-knit it was, and it certainly played a part in my journey. But I have always viewed places as stepping-stones. If you stay in one place for too long, you're not moving forward. You are not evolving. Life is moving forward, and you are getting left behind. There must be a reason why some people constantly seek variation and change as they maneuver through their lives. The more I learned, the more I experienced, the wider my thoughts would range. That curiosity has always fueled my life and was the impetus for my journey.

I always wondered if there was something out there

that could fill a void that even home could not fill. I equated it to my justification for why people moved out of the comfort of their family homes. For me, it was the insatiable desire to become independent, someone who had the means to take care of herself and extend a helping hand toward those around her. I wanted to know self-actualization, and I wanted to instigate it as a core value in other people who may have settled for their current state and become too comfortable to consider anything else.

That is precisely why I valued the trips my father and I often took to visit the airport. I was always curious about what existed beyond our view of the universe, and I wanted to envision the various possibilities of experiences around the world. I wanted to know where the planes went once the sky engulfed them.

My father was always supportive of my dreams, being a leader rather than a follower himself. While he worked hard to support his family, he enjoyed listening to my dreams and felt content in the knowledge that he would see the brave and ambitious parts of himself live out in my dreams. I often wondered if some people's lack of goals led to the decreased inspiration to dream. Or perhaps some people do not have goals that inspire them. I have come to learn that you must seek inspiration before you seek anything else. As I imparted this information to my protégé, another flashback ensued.

When we were young, my mother brushed my sister's hair a hundred times every night. I wondered why Mommy never brushed my hair. I always wanted to be popular and pretty like my sister, but I was an introvert, not the type to like crowds or follow popular people around. I always felt invisible and overlooked. Somehow, I convinced myself I was all right feeling that way.

As I offered the protégé some juice, I told her about one of my realizations during a trip to the airport with my father. I didn't want to settle for the life that had been predefined for me. To leverage an airplane metaphor, I wanted to be seated on the plane instead of being the one who watched it fly away. I wanted to see as much of the world as I could. What I really wanted was to find a way to inspire people to dream beyond their circumstances. I wanted to make a difference in people's lives and be a source of inspiration for anyone who was looking for that small bit of motivation to hold onto their dreams. For me, it was not always easy. Because of my family dynamics, I never felt the warmth and unconditional love that I yearned for.

Somehow, I had developed an expectation of what a family should feel like, and for me, it never felt quite right. I watched other families interact with one another. Some were far less loving than mine, and others were far more loving than mine. I had developed an idea of what motherly love was supposed to be like, and I desired that kind of unconditional love that I thought would be natural and present in the one person I thought should always believe in me. I expected unconditional love, the kind that would genuinely cause my family to believe in me and support my dreams.

My mother always said she loved me, but it never felt like the same love she gave my sister. I could see the love and adoration she doted on my sister. In comparison, with me, it felt like she said she loved me because it was the right thing to say. Visits to my maternal grandparents felt that way too—like they accepted us and tolerated us but didn't love us and would have preferred not to have us around. It was odd watching our cousins get showered with love while we felt like outsiders.

I never understood the power dynamics at play with the adults. Over the years, things became clearer as I started to understand more of what was at play. My immediate family were the outsiders. We were the ones that were not part of the internal fabric that was woven through the extended family because my father wasn't part of the clique. Scenarios in their childhood had drawn a wedge between dad, mom and some of their siblings. We, my siblings and I, were being raised into the inauthentic remnants of a family struggling to mend old wounds. As I experienced this during my formative years, it taught me many things. I decided that I did not want pretense and superficiality in my life. I would always make sure people saw me for who I was instead of whether I fit their predefined mold of what I should or should not be. It was difficult not receiving love from my primary caregiver, always being told one thing and feeling another. It led to a lot of self-doubts, and I questioned my worth at times. If my mother did not approve of me, how would the rest of the world? She was supposedly the person who knew me best; after all, she had given birth to me. I realized this was a notion of seeking self-admiration that society had me believe, and above all else, I needed to figure out who I was. I needed to seek internal acceptance and admiration rather than looking for it to come from an external source. The best part about it was that I would be constructing a mold instead of being restricted to a preconstructed one. And I could set this mold to be as large as I aspired instead of limiting my growth. I just needed the courage to build that path for myself since there was no precedent. I could be curious beyond boundaries and limits—if I had the courage.

Chapter 4

CHILDHOOD MEMORIES

THE PROTÉGÉ INQUIRED MORE ABOUT MY childhood, and I shared one of my fond memories—dropping by Ms. Francis's place after school. Ms. Francis took care of the children in the neighborhood while our parents were busy at their jobs. I always thought Ms. Francis was such a presence of a woman. She was tall and stout, and my mother was so petite. I loved melting into her embrace and taking in the scent of all the items she cooked daily in her home that latched onto her apron. She defined day care for us, as we didn't have a traditional day care system. Her caring, kindness, and devotion have stayed with me all these years.

All of the children usually finished homework at Ms. Francis's place. When we were allowed, we would play hide-and-seek or spend hours having fun keeping ourselves occupied in the hall where we all played. We were content in our little bubble of bliss, and I grew up to realize that even ignorance is bliss. Our neighborhood was secure, and we never had anything to fear; you only fear that which you do not know. In taking the risk to step out of my comfort zone, I soon realized that a plethora of pleasant experiences accompanied this fear, and the first fear I had to overcome was that of fear itself.

In our neighborhood, everything felt familiar and safe. We played games on our block, almost always in the street, because we didn't have sprawling lawns or large yards. We played kickball, tag, and dodge ball. Sometimes we made up games to play. I recall something we called *running bases*. It was a game that was equal parts tag and catch. I remember that game because it was the first time I learned how to use a baseball glove. I had to learn to use my nondominant hand to catch so I could use my dominant hand to throw. I was quite good at catching, and I learned to be ambidextrous with the glove because I could not understand how you could be good at the game unless both hands could perform as dominant.

We knew we were supposed to return home once the streetlights came on, because we did not stay out past dark. In the evenings, my father and I would venture out to the airport, where we found blinking lights in the darkness. We would drive to the top level of the parking garage where we had a direct view of the airport runways. When the weather was nice, we would sit on the hood of the car and watch planes arriving and departing. If he had not allowed me to go out with him after dark, I would have never known how beautiful the blinking lights of airplanes looked against the nighttime sky.

My father and I had such a wonderful time together that it never bothered me that I had heard him say how he had wanted a son when I was born. He embraced me as his baby girl and taught me a love of sports, and I quickly became enamored with my father as my best friend. Daddy soon realized that his little girl enjoyed the activities a son would have enjoyed. My father had wanted a little sidekick, and I became that for him—a mini version of him, someone who loved all the same things he did. My personality mirrored his and I inherited his ambition. We talked about sports and played in the yard when he came home from work. When his schedule allowed, he indulged in quiet drives alone, which he called his thinking time. On some evenings, when the sky was clear, he would plan to drive to the airport and would allow me to join him to watch planes. This is when I established my love for watching planes. It was on one such night, many years later, that I told my father about my desire to explore a chance at an education that would create opportunities for me that were different from the traditional route our family had taken.

I didn't want to follow my family to the factory jobs; I wanted something different. I had no idea what that entailed precisely, at first. But my father told me I had taken the first and most rudimental step to success—daring to dream. I wanted him to know I felt guilty for not being happy with the circumstances at hand but that I was determined to figure it out, and determination is one value he could wholeheartedly appreciate. What I really wanted was his blessing. I wanted him to tell me it was OK. I wanted his support and to know that he believed in me. At the time, that was all I really needed. I needed to know my father was proud. Tears brimmed my eyes as a nostalgia-clad memory made its way into my mind …

"Daddy," I said, looking up at him with a teary, doe-eyed expression, "is it wrong to dream of being a pilot if people like us do not even dream of flying?"

He held my hand in his and looked me in the eye, as he had so many times before, then simply said, "Look around you. What do you see? You see Daddy, you see this runway, and you see the airport. You can see a few trees, and that's it. Now imagine what someone sees when they look at this landscape from up there in the sky. They can see the runway, the tops of these trees, the entire neighborhood, and so much more. They can even see the clouds. There wouldn't have been an invention of an airplane if someone hadn't wanted to explore the sky. Never fear to be extraordinary. Embrace the desire to take flight and vanish from vision.

Daddy's words came as a relief to me. If people around me did not accept me, that would be because of their limited views of the possibilities around us and their reluctance to change. Since everything in this world is dynamic, we might as well choose a path that leads to evolution.

Chapter 5

REFLECTION AND REALIZATION

As I snapped back to reality, I let my young guest know that this resolve to change strengthened when I realized the people who had the most money in our neighborhood were into questionable activities. In fact, these activities were the most common ways people in our community gained affluence. I didn't understand how they made so much money because I didn't understand who had that much money to give to them. What I *did* understand very clearly is that these were extremely lucrative businesses. Those who indulged in these activities had the nicest cars, wore the nicest jewelry, and were the most popular people in town. Everyone knew who they were, and everyone respected them. We all idolized them, and many of us wanted to live the lives they lived.

Most of these individuals in our neighborhood were people we had spent our childhoods with, which is why it was not as alarming as it would have been in another community. While this was one way to have wealth, and many people from our neighborhood were into the game, it was not something I wanted to do. My goal was to get an education and have opportunities that would get me out of the neighborhood. What I came to realize was that these were smart people who ran elaborate businesses. Based on everything I now know about business models and operational management, I realize the significance of those enterprises. There was always a complicated supply chain. There were sophisticated logistics and distribution channels. There was a robust client relationship management (CRM) system. And most importantly, there was a significant compensation process with a recognition and rewards program.

I would talk to my friends and try to figure out what was really going on. They always tried to shield me from the details to keep me out of the inner loop. Now I realize they were keeping me on the legal side of the information flow. I didn't understand it when I was younger. But now I know why they didn't tell me everything. What I do understand is that they had a command on finance, economics, product management, client and market analytics, talent development, promotions, and talent management—all of which they learned from the streets. To me, they were brilliant business people who learned to manage their business enterprises the best way they knew how, considering the restrictions life had placed on them. I wanted to be smart, and I wanted to run a business, but I wanted to take a different route. I wanted financial security, and I wanted to earn respect. I knew I was not cut out for the life I saw them living. While I wanted the success, I wanted to go about things a different way.

The protégé then inquired about the process I went through when figuring out the route I wanted to take. I told her about the day I stumbled across an advertisement about flying school. I smiled at the thought of my father appreciating my desire to set a clear goal and aim for exactly what I wanted. He was proud I didn't assume I had to become a flight attendant, because during those times, there were few if any women pilots, and roles for women were more narrowly defined. Yet I was comfortable putting the pilot seat in range for myself. I would not be bound by what was expected or what had been. I had my sights on what could be—regardless of what was expected or what boundaries had historically been defined.

As I explored this possibility, I decided that I did not want to be a commercial airline pilot. While I loved watching planes and enjoyed the idea of traveling on airplanes, I realized the concept of becoming a pilot was more of a metaphor for wanting to be in the driver's seat of my life, with no boundaries. I wanted to reach the clouds. That was my dream. I decided education would be the way to expand beyond my current environment.

The foundation of this dream lay in the fact that nobody from my extended family had graduated with a college degree. This was also probably why nobody understood why I wanted to take that route; moreover, no one apart from my father believed I could accomplish it. Many of these lessons are musings in retrospect; during those times, I often felt disillusioned and lost. I had to figure out everything from scratch because, while my father was supportive, he did not know much beyond the reality of his experiences. A world of possibilities was awaiting me, but I did not know how to approach them. I had taken the first step in building the willpower, but I was embarking on a journey on an unfamiliar path that no one from my immediate environment had traveled.

Pathways that people often travel are easy to navigate,

because either the imprints of the footsteps of your predecessors are visible to guide you, or you can easily ask any other person who is familiar with the route. Finding a new pathway means you are stepping into the dark. There are no streetlights there because no one you know has made a visit to the place, and there may not even be a well-constructed path. You do not see what creatures the shrubbery holds, and you have to be vigilant to ensure you do not trip and fall into a ditch that you did not even know was present because no one could warn you about it. It is important to unlock yourself from fear of disappointment and fear of the unknown. This may seem scary, but focus on all that you may be missing out on if you give into the fear and do not explore your dreams.

The curious protégé asked me to elaborate on my motivations behind seeking a life different from those around me. This made me pause, and I wondered about the various driving forces in my life. I had always been curious. I had always believed that there is an abundance of knowledge in the world and that even if I spent my entire lifetime learning, I would still miss out on certain lessons. My thirst for knowledge was unquenchable. But it would be difficult to do justice to all the driving forces in my life. I guess one way of looking at it would be—if there was a chance to do something different, why not try? Why not explore as many options as I could, even those that were unknown to me?

I saw people around me living a simple, complacent life. I remember Daddy going upstairs to pay rent to our landlord, Mr. Curry. Of course, I tagged along, because why not tag along? I overheard them talking about how Mr. Curry had sold the house and we would have to move. I was confused. What did that mean? How could he tell us we had to move from our home? This confused me, so I waited until later in the day to explore my curiosity. Daddy was always forthcoming with me. He allowed me to be inquisitive and explained things in a way I could understand. I asked, "What is rent?" I learned there was a difference between paying rent and owning the house. And I wondered, *Why does one choose to pay rent if they intend to stay in the space forever? What is the value in that? Why not have a place you can call your own?* My juvenile curiosity made my mind wonder, and I added to my list of one-day-I-want-to-have items. I wanted to have a place I could call my own. Having a place of my own would be an investment that would show that I had made my place in the world, a more lasting one. And while I appreciated the hard work people around me demonstrated in their daily jobs,

I wanted to be in a position where I had the power to call more of the shots in my life. I didn't want to be a tenant, at the mercy of someone else's decisions. I wanted to be the landlord of my life.

So, I began asking myself how I could be different. I realized I could not control what I was born into or my current environment. Nor could I control the set of opportunities that were present for me. But I could surely control where I went from there. And there were so many places I wanted to go to. I would have to create or seek out an opportunity that would fit my needs.

The factors that I could control were my education and the networks I made. I could also expand my environment beyond the current scope of space and opportunity. During our airport adventures, I realized the only vacations people around me took were those to visit their families. I knew that would never be enough for me. I wanted to work hard, watch my initiatives evolve into solutions for real-time problems, and then take well-deserved vacations all around the globe. I needed exposure before all else and then a legitimate way to make money to spend on experiences that would further nurture my growth into a well-rounded individual.

Chapter 6

MICHAEL, MY MOTIVATION

ONE OF THE PRIMARY MOTIVATIONS FOR ME to evolve was the heartfelt love I harbored for my brother and his consistent encouragement. I told the protégé more about my brother, as he played a significant role in my life.

When I was five years old, on April 27, the universe answered Daddy's prayers for a son and gave me a little brother, the sweetest little boy—someone to love. Mommy let me give him his middle name, and I named him after a boy I liked in school. I remember the call from the hospital and choosing the name. It seems like it was yesterday. The phone cord was so short that I had to stand by the nightstand in their bedroom. It's odd how my mind has held on to that memory for so many years.

I liked watching Michael grow. He was smart and

curious but easily influenced. He wanted to know everything from the moment he learned to talk, and he had a lot of questions. This was one thing we had in common, one that made us feel closer to each other. I would tell him things and then send him to Mommy and Daddy for clarification. We got into a lot of trouble together.

I recall Michael's first day of school. My sister and I picked out his clothes. We had talked Mommy into buying him a pair of penny loafers, and we had bought him a pair of light copper-colored pants that had pennies on the pockets. We were so excited to dress him and take him to school with us. But Michael wasn't pleased about going to school. When he realized he would have to be there alone, fear came over his face, and he didn't want to leave. Our house had a chain-link fence, and he wrapped his fingers around the fence for dear life. We had to peel his little fingers from around the metal one at a time and ensure him he would be OK. We were all crying so much because no matter what we said, the fear in him would not release. Up to that moment, he trusted us, but we could not get him to believe us. At one point, he looked right at me with a look of disbelief that I would be making him do this. I quietly whispered, "Trust me. It's OK." He kept crying, but he let go, and we left to walk around the corner to our school. After school, I asked how it was. His response was one word—good. That was all he had to say about school. But he was ready to go the next day. When I think about peeling his little fingers off the fence and forcing him to encounter the unknown, it still brings tears to my eyes.

I enjoyed having my brother around because he made me think. We would pretend *what if* all of the time. What if we lived somewhere else? What if we were super rich? What if I was a pilot? Or an important business person who traveled to faraway places for work? We would laugh and remind ourselves these were just thoughts and dreams, things beyond our reach.

One day while we were watching TV, he asked me, "What would it take for us to have the things we pretend about?" I had already been curious about that. Our parents worked hard. We had a nice home. We had a good life. It was better than how they grew up. It seemed similar to the lives of all the people around us. I didn't want to appear ungrateful for their struggles and sacrifices. I knew they worked extremely hard. They worked a lot. At an early age, I was observant and aware. I saw how much they worked. We had everything we needed. And for the most part, we had everything we wanted too.

The thing I really wanted could not be purchased. In these moments, I was getting that thing—the love and support of my little brother, who was always in awe of his big sister. I desired to be different, and what I needed was someone to believe I could make it happen and to give me the inspiration to follow my dreams. Daddy believed I would do it. Michael inspired me to want to do it. The universe gave me not only a little brother but someone to inspire and motivate me. He was my catalyst. My rock. My heart and soul. He believed in me. He encouraged me. He was always there for me.

After I graduated from high school, I became the first one from the family to go to college. When I got my first job after college, and later when I fulfilled my dream of working on Wall Street. Michael was always there as my biggest cheerleader. At one point, as he was deciding on his post–high school life, Michael was feeling the pressure of the family boundaries. It was customary for the family to go to work in the factory our parents worked in. Many of our cousins followed that path. He didn't want to do that. He wasn't sure what he wanted to do, but he wanted the ability to make his own decisions without the pressure and scrutiny of the family. He watched how I maneuvered, and he wanted to find his own way, as I had done. I wanted to be supportive of him because I realized how important those moments were for me. Michael found his way and settled into his career choice. Along the way, we kept each other focused, committed, and grounded, never letting the other feel alone or discouraged—and never allowing either of us to get complacent.

As I moved away from our home state, alone, to take a job in another state more than six hundred miles away, he encouraged me. He came to visit. As I built my first house, from a hole in the ground, he was there every step of the way, helping me fulfill my dream—our dream—of homeownership. No more rent! He helped me make decisions about everything from the exterior elevation to the interior flooring. We shared those moments and watched our dream become a reality. He was a rock for everyone. A supporter. An encourager. A friend. He was by my side when we lost our father. Then again when we lost our sister. Both suddenly and unexpectedly. Both extremely sad.

He was always there. Until he was gone. One tragic night, a car accident took him away, and with him, a part of my heart and soul that would never be replaced. If I had to identify the point in my life when I was at my lowest, it would be Sunday, April 20, 2008, at 3:15 a.m. At that moment, on Route 78 in Warren, New

Jersey, my brother lost his life. At that moment, I lost my inspiration, my focus, and my purpose. I sank. I balled myself up and cried. I cried for days. I couldn't understand. I wanted to understand. Nothing made sense anymore. Nothing mattered. All of our dreams, our plans, our goals … We were supposed to do so many things together. He had made me believe our dreams were within reach. I couldn't imagine how I was supposed to move forward without his love, without his support, without him cheering me along the journey. I believed life was over.

One night, in a dream, Michael told me nothing I did would change what happened, so I could not wallow in the grief. That dream that night set me back on our course. I was alone, but I was not lonely anymore. I could then, and still do now, feel his love and support guiding me through the decisions I made in life.

As I reflect on this, the protégé sees me smile and witnesses the connection I still have with Michael. He is always with me, and that is my forever source of inspiration.

That tragedy left me with the desire to always remember our promises. Never give up. Never accept less than we think we deserve in any situation. Never settle for what life is handing us.

I guess that is my primary driving force; the desire to continually make my little brother, Michael, proud fuels my every move. Every decision I make and every action I take is done with one question in my mind: what would Michael want me to do? He would never want me to be afraid. He would always want me to be courageous and unapologetic. He would want me to remain optimistic about success, to dream big enough to make my fears seem small in comparison. He is always with me, always challenging me, questioning my thoughts, comforting my fears. I smile every time I think of him, and I quietly celebrate every success—big or small—with him.

Chapter 7

VULNERABILITY AND AUTHENTICITY

THE SOBERING YET ENCOURAGING DISCUSSION about my brother brought tears to the protégé's eyes. She told me she never would have imagined I was silently carrying that level of grief with me all the time. She said that she had approached this discussion, wishing she could have my life, that my smile was bright enough to light a room. She said that she felt positive energy while she talked to me, but she could not have imagined the extent of the grief I had encountered. I told her I knew what she meant and that it is easy to look at me today and think my path has been smooth.

What people don't see very often—because I have mastered the ability to perfect the fake smile, because I have learned how to push the sad feelings away, because

I have learned how to successfully hide the grief that consistently overwhelms me and oftentimes consumes my thoughts—is the broken little girl. The person who has never really felt what a mother's unconditional love and support feels like. The person who came to terms with the reality of her life a long time ago. Grief does not vanish one day; more often than not, it is here to stay. Some days, it can completely consume you, and other days it's like a fleeting thought. But it's there every minute of every day. I have learned to use that intensity of emotion as the fuel for my purpose. Everyone has a why. The dreams Michael and I had are my why.

At this point, I conveyed a heartfelt sentiment to my protégé. You are the only one who cares about the things you care about in the way you care about them. You are the only one who will make the life you want possible. You are responsible for yourself. If you fail, it's your fault. Never play the victim game, even when the odds are stacked against you. Stop looking for someone to understand. Stop looking for someone to help. Stop looking for someone to care. Start learning. Start exploring. Start expanding your reach. Start believing in yourself. Start doing—something. Anything. Just start! Unlock the secrets to your success.

But first I needed to define my version of success.

Today, someone can look at me and think it was easy. Think I am happy. Think I am put together. My mask hides it all. My response to people who say they want my life is "You don't want my life. You want your life. You must first believe that you can have whatever life you dream of." And that is what I said to the protégé.

After I said, "You can," I corrected myself to say, "You *will*—if you commit to your success." I further elaborated that I was telling my story in the hope that it would encourage others to recognize their potential and their truth and unlock their inspiration. My brother always believed in me even when I didn't believe in myself. He encouraged me, pushed me to do more, to try harder. He gave me hope when I was down, and he showed me the bond of family that I always longed for. I want to play a similar role in the lives of those who do not have someone by their side, or who are at a loss regarding the next steps along their path to success, or who feel as if the journey is lonely and need encouragement from someone who understands how that feels.

PART II

THE HUSTLE: ROADS LESS TRAVELED

Chapter 8

VALUE OF ENCOURAGEMENT

As the protégé and I snacked on some chocolates, I shared a lesson I carried from my childhood into adulthood: the company you keep matters. Surround yourself with people who encourage and foster your growth, and use your newfound skills and exposure to help those around you who need a little push to tap into the potential they possess. The first person to believe in me, apart from my father and my brother, was Ms. Branch. Her name is quite apt to my story because I think she is the first person outside of my family who gave me hope that my dreams could transform into reality, that I could branch out and bloom into the best version of myself.

I was in fifth grade when I had the pleasure of being taught by Ms. Branch. She found ways around the curriculum because she saw that I was learning at a faster pace than some of my classmates. Somehow, she recognized I was not being challenged enough, so she began to offer me extra material once I finished the set curriculum. She was one of the many people in my life who extended a helping hand to me while desiring nothing in return. I believe such people are the driving force behind real success in the world. I learned very early on that you need to mingle with the kind of crowd that does not aim to succeed at your expense but instead believes in joining hands to envision futures and solutions like never before. As I told the eager protégé about my life lessons, I was transported to another flashback.

"I finished the assignment, Ms. Branch," I said, looking at my teacher with a giant smile plastered across my face. Her constant appreciation provided me with the validation I needed to finish my work much earlier than my classmates. I always enjoyed the extra coursework she presented to me.

Ms. Branch made me feel different in such a good way. I felt special because she encouraged me to work harder and to learn more. She gave me books with interesting characters, and I learned additional facts. I felt lucky when Ms. Branch would show her commitment to my education, and her enthusiasm fueled my animated interest.

As I snapped back to reality, I decided to talk about my transition into high school and how I struggled with being different. When I was in junior high school, it occurred to me that being popular meant fitting in, something I was opposed to. Becoming successful meant doing things differently, and I needed to accept that. The funny thing is when you're stepping out of your comfort zone or the set standards in your community, people have a lot to say about it. But once you're successful, the very same people begin paying attention and start respecting you. However, there are still going to be some people who will lash out because of the animosity they feel toward all that you are trying to achieve. It is essential to come to terms with the fact that you will not be able to please everyone if you want to try to be successful. There are those who will try to take advantage of your success. The kind of people you should seek are those who recognize your potential and who wish to blaze a trail for the merits of your hard work to yield the results you aspire to reach—those who seek to help you achieve success as you have defined it for yourself.

One such person for me was my junior high school guidance counselor, who informed me about the entrance exam for University High School. I juggled with the idea of trying to go to a better high school so that I could gain an education that would adequately equip me for the future I dreamt of. It was a tough decision to make because I was going to be separated from all of my friends. I would be taking a step that people were not supportive of. When I attempted the test to gain admission into the school, most people were either unsupportive or indifferent. Others were coming from a selfish place because they did not want me to leave so that we could continue to spend our school days together. Nobody truly understood how essential this step was for my growth, even if it meant commuting to a different neighborhood to study. Since higher education had never been a priority for those around me, I found myself at the receiving end of a lot of negative energy.

I took a leap of faith and went to take the test anyway, and I was over-the-moon filled with excitement when I passed. A lot of people, including my sister, remarked that I was trying to be better than them, but I just wanted them to understand that I was simply trying to be me. The response from my sister was interesting, considering all of my life everyone had made sure to let me know I was so much less than her. I had given up trying to be considered as anything other than insignificant compared to her.

Choosing a high school was certainly a defining

moment in my life because it marked the time when I finally began mingling with people from beyond my neighborhood. Of course, this was not an easy transition. At first, I could not believe how different the setting was. My peers at the new school had parents who were more successful than anyone's parents I knew personally in my neighborhood. I struggled with feelings of inadequacy, like I didn't belong there with them. Those feelings that had been instilled in me kept reappearing. But I kept reminding myself that I had made it based on my merit and that I deserved a place in the school. This was the first step in making a space for myself in the new environment.

Initially, I found the students to be super nerdy and corny. They were so studious and different from the kids in my neighborhood, and it was certainly a major change. I couldn't understand it or explain it, but they were very different. The kids in my neighborhood used to come to the school to be a nuisance to the students attending my current school. It was odd to watch the differences play out in that manner, and I had to decide where I would fit in.

I missed my friends at my old school. Sometimes the immense pressure to perform well in the competitive environment of my new school overwhelmed me. Then

I thought about how the most precious stones are formed under immense amounts of pressure and how it was honing my capabilities and my ability to perform well.

Moreover, the school prepared me for the real world because the real world consists of people from all walks of life, and you need to learn how to make a place for yourself amid them while learning about various cultures simultaneously. This was the first time I truly stood out. I was surrounded by smart peers, and I chose to be friends with people who challenged me intellectually but made me feel comfortable at the same time. While I was learning how to fit in, I realized I was more comfortable just being myself rather than trying to emulate those around me. My genuine self is curious and kind of comical. I can be intense, and I don't like being confused. I let my curiosity and my humor carry me through the days, and I remained true to my genuine character.

This made me more comfortable learning new things and studying with those who were much more intellectually advanced than I was. I thought I was smart, but I was learning what it really meant to be smart. This taught me a very valuable lesson; it's easy to be the best in a room where you are not challenged. The true test of your worth is when you surround yourself with people who are better than you are.

How do you learn to survive in those moments? That was a lesson I had to quickly adapt to if I was going to survive. The closest group of friends in my circle consisted of the future valedictorian and the salutatorian. I was in the top three, and that made me feel proud. I had earned my spot among what I considered the elite. As I look back on it now, I made some close friends who are still my friends today. We still laugh together, support each other, challenge each other to be great, and cheer for each other's success—big ones and small ones. Our bond was built on a common goal—to be our best. And for a few of us, that bond is still as strong today as it was then.

I think this is an apt time to mention that when I first joined my new school, I was delighted that one of my best friends from my neighborhood joined as well. It felt good not being alone during the transition, and somebody would understand the dilemmas my background posed. Nicole and I had developed such a great friendship over the years; we were more like sisters than friends. But she did not like the school. She also thought it was corny. In addition, she did not enjoy the immense amount of work, and it was understandable because expectations at the new school were entirely different from anything we had ever been exposed to. We were expected to maintain a certain GPA if we wanted to do well, and the classes were far more demanding than the schooling system we had been a part of.

Nicole left soon after joining, and I think she wanted me to follow suit. But I was finally headed in a direction that could lead me to the kind of success I envisioned for myself, and I knew it was not going to come easily. I would need to grow a thicker skin if I wanted to expose myself to unfamiliar atmospheres and environments. I think my biggest challenge during this time was navigating how to feel accepted and worthy at the same time. But it was the first time I started believing that I was preparing for something bigger and that I had the requisite skills and opportunities to do so. I unlocked the motivations that set me apart and embraced them instead of shying away from them, and that made all the difference for me.

Chapter 9

CHARTING MY COURSE

I IMPLORE UPON THE IMPORTANCE OF STANDING by decisions that allow you to grow. Such choices usually put us through a degree of turmoil, but we emerge successful and more aware of their aftermath. A decision is not a one-off choice you make; you need to actively stick by the pact you have made with yourself every single day to unlock your potential. I made the decision that I did not want to compromise on the quality of my education, which was the reason I made a commitment to attend University High School instead of my neighborhood school.

While I am confident I could have received a quality education, my desire to expand beyond what was comfortable and familiar was the reason for selecting an advanced high school education. As a result, I was fortunate enough to be introduced to an organization that would prepare me for a future I had only dreamed of before.

I quickly learned that organization would be the catalyst to propel me into my future. But first, I needed to choose a career path. I was once again in unfamiliar territory. I had no knowledge of careers in corporate America. I also had no one in my family or neighborhood I could seek guidance from. How could I choose a career path when I had no clue what options were available? I had no exposure to anyone who had a corporate career. I leveraged my new network for assistance. After many discussions about the things I liked, the subjects I preferred in school, my dreams of what the perfect job would be, and the need to establish a clear path toward the level of compensation I wanted to experience, I landed on accounting as my career choice. This choice helped me plan for a college major in accounting.

The organization immediately began to prepare me for the journey. As I embarked on this intense preparation, I made friends with the other students who were also beginning in the program. There were weekend classes during my senior year of high school. I cannot say we enjoyed it much. I recall our executive director reminding us that we had been selected for the program. He said if we were not willing to make the commitment, we could leave and let someone else occupy our seat. That set the tone for many weekend sessions, and I knew I would invest myself in the process wholeheartedly. Our group became a close-knit team of students from across the region, focused solely on gaining the insights necessary to plan our futures.

When we were ready, or should I say ready enough, the organization set us up with interviews with Fortune 500 companies. The roles were strategically aligned with our career choices and pending college majors. We supported and encouraged one another as we all prepared for interviews. In many instances, we were competing with one another as well. We welcomed this and let it help us challenge one another.

During this process, we learned a valuable lesson: it is all right to compete when everyone is supportive of the outcome. In this case, we knew the person who was the best prepared and who made the best impression would probably get selected. We each worked diligently to be well prepared, and we knew the rest would be fate. We would be happy for one another and supportive of the outcomes.

During the interview process, I felt so unprepared. Even though we had worked hard on our mock interviews, something about walking into those amazingly beautiful office buildings and meeting immaculately dressed business professionals who spoke proper English and sounded so smart made me feel uncomfortable. The fear of not being worthy of occupying the space crept in, and the tall buildings and self-assured individuals were intimidating. It was unnerving and could have thrown me off my game. I kept reminding myself I deserved to be in this situation and that growth was supposed to feel uncomfortable at first. While I was hyperventilating inside, I managed my way through the interviews.

I second-guessed myself. Did I respond appropriately? Did I present the right impression? Did I ask intelligent questions? Was I able to articulate how well I had studied the company? I beat myself up over anything I could. Imagine my surprise when I learned I had done well in all of the interviews—so well, in fact, that I was offered an internship with seven of the eight companies I interviewed with. Of course, I was focused on the one that didn't make me an offer and let that impact my ability to celebrate the moment. When I overcame those feelings, I was pleasantly surprised, but at the same time, I was even more afraid. If I had not been accepted, I could have fallen back on my comfort zone of familiarity. But I had come too far, and this made it all very real.

I was face-to-face with the opportunity I had worked so hard for. I was being given a chance to change my life, and there was no way I was going to mess this up. Now, how was I supposed to choose? For me, there was only one way to differentiate, and that was who made me feel like I could belong there. All of the organizations would provide excellent opportunities. All were good companies at the top of their industry. But something about the people I met at one company made me feel as if I would be given a chance to learn and grow. I know now that it was the culture that made me comfortable. I will elaborate further on this later.

Chapter 10

TRANSITION TO COLLEGE

THE INTERNSHIP STARTED THE SUMMER before I left for college. It allowed me to experience the subject materials I would be presented with in my college classes. Leaving for college was a big deal, as I was the first one in my family to actually go to college. And I chose to go to school out of state, to a place my family had never been. I was excited, but I was also nervous. I was starting to be filled with doubt. Could I do it? Would I be OK? How would I feel? I knew I would once again have to make new friends all over again.

Now that college was becoming a real thing, my family was beginning to be a bit more accepting, even supportive. Everyone in the family had chipped in to make sure I had everything I needed for my dorm, and

I felt grateful for such pockets of wholesomeness. From pillows to comforters to school supplies, everything I could think of had been given to me. Even though none of us understood what I was about to go through, it seemed that everyone was at least supportive in the moment. It felt like a normal, functioning family unit. My mother and my aunt loaded the car to drive the eight hours to my college. I think we were all excited and anxious. I remember wondering if I was ready for what was to come.

I had visited the school only once, on a campus tour, and I had immediately fallen in love with the environment. I felt comfortable. Once I arrived, I was in for a new experience. My roommate was a young woman from Puerto Rico. English was her second language. There were only a few ethnically diverse women in my dorm. For all of us, this was the first time living away from home. The women of the ethnic majority in our dorm shared stories of boarding schools and international family trips to help us get acclimated so we would not be homesick. It was an awareness of life outside of my home, my neighborhood, and my city that made me learn how to live on my own.

Early in the semester, one of my dormmates from across the hall had family come to visit. I recall it vividly.

I was walking out of my room to head to the stairs to go to the main building for lunch. My friend was coming from the stairs to go to her room, which was right across the hall from me. She had her little brother with her. When he saw me, he ran away, screaming. We did not know why. Her family calmed him, and we both went our separate ways. Later that night, she told me that he had never seen a Black person before. He, therefore, with his limited experience and exposure to anyone who was not White, thought I was a bear. And he was afraid of bears. So, he did what anyone would do. He ran.

While this was odd to me, I understood. I had never lived amongst mostly white people before. It was frightening for me, too, but in a very different kind of way. In addition, I had many bears in my life as well—assignments I was not used to and work pressures I was still getting accustomed to. The incident made me realize how important it was for me to take the first step in making sure it became a norm to see people of all colors succeeding.

College was a complete shift in life for me. I was there to learn, and I was prepared for that part. What I was not prepared for were the life changes. I knew I would meet new people. I knew I would have new experiences. But I did not have any way to understand what that meant until I was thrown into it. And I didn't have anyone to help prepare me for it in the way I needed to understand it. Remember, I was the first from my family to go to college. While I asked a lot of questions during my internship, the people I was asking had come from families where college was a normal part of their lineage. So, their perspectives on readiness and preparation were not as useful for me. And I was a long way from home now. So, I had to figure it out.

My roommate was named Nancy. She and I were polar opposites. As I mentioned, Nancy spoke English as her second language. While she was fluent in English, it took her time to process. It was normal for me to talk fast. That was how we talked in my life. Nancy was an extreme introvert. She did not have friends, and she did not want friends. I am an introvert, but I wanted to make friends. So, I tried to meet some of the other people in the dorm. I figured that if we had to live together for a year, we might as well get to know one another.

I was not looking for a best friend; I just wanted some familiarity and comfort. It was my first time being away from home, and it was a strange and unfamiliar environment for me. I was from an inner city, and this was not that. But I couldn't help where I was from and how I was raised. So, the natural instinct in me was to survey my surroundings and be comfortable.

Nancy was not interested. She had come from a high-class suburb. Her family was full of doctors who had stellar educations. She was extremely nice, but she was not interested in friendship. The cultural variances were obvious from day one. Everyone left their doors open as a way to be welcoming to others while we were getting introduced. I was not comfortable with that at first; it took some getting used to. Then it seemed normal. People would come in to say hello and introduce themselves. Nancy would be extremely short with them. I, however, was interested in learning about the people we were living with.

Who were these people, and where did they come from? Nancy would close the door. I would leave it open. Navigating a middle ground while living with someone was our first lesson, especially if you did not know them. This lesson reminded me of a few things. Before school started, we had been assigned our roommates. My colleagues at the internship had advised me to be sure to reach out to her to start getting to know her before we left for school. I had tried and realized she did not seem friendly. That created a significant level of discomfort for me as I prepared to embark on my college journey. Now

I was beginning to see this play out in real life. Nancy was fun, and she was very friendly. I realized she was just not comfortable getting to know new people because she did not want to struggle with the cultural variances any more than she had to. She was in school to get her education, and that was all. I decided I was not going to try to change her. We had fun studying together. We liked to read, which gave us our space in our dorm room. I decorated my side of the room with all the things I liked. She did not do any decorations. We coexisted in our space and didn't get in each other's way.

I met a few other ethnically diverse individuals during my first few weeks, and we became friends. I realized that for many, college life was a social experience. For me, it was more of a learning experience. Learning to live differently. Learning to be comfortable in unfamiliar spaces. Learning how to fit in. Learning how not to feel inadequate. I always felt like I did not belong, and I was grappling with that unsettling feeling. While I was enjoying the experience, I felt like I was different. I was not popular. I was not pretty. I just was. I wanted to learn what set me apart.

I had a group of friends at a school nearby who were from my neighborhood back home. I spent most of my time outside of school work with them. It was safe, and it was familiar. A short bus ride put me right into the comfort of my old life. They were just a year ahead of me, and they had made a comfortable space for themselves. And they welcomed me in. That made a huge difference for me. A level of familiarity while exploring so many new fronts was a necessity.

I was a tutor on campus for math and accounting subjects. I enjoyed helping others. I was able to grasp the subject matter pretty well, and I felt good about that. My high school education had been extremely beneficial. The things Mrs. White taught us at University High School were the same things I was learning in my English classes, freshman year. That made the course work easy to grasp. I did not have any issues with those classes.

However, I did have issues with one subject. I totally struggled with econ classes, and I do not know why. It took me a while to understand the concepts, but in the end, I grew to love the concepts and leveraged them in my career. It made me process that you can turn your weaknesses into your strengths with the right amount of effort. This was another example of how some things would be easier than others. Every part of life presents us with something to learn. How we embrace the struggle and how we face the challenge determines how we move past that phase of life. Econ classes were a speedbump on a smoothly paved road. If I had treated it like a roadblock or given it more power than it had, I could have experienced my college education differently. Instead, I focused and built a plan to conquer the challenge.

Chapter 11

THE INTERNSHIP

THE INTERNSHIP I CHOSE WAS AT A PUBLIC accounting firm. It was one of the Big Eight at the time. I got the opportunity to see CPAs in action. I had real-time exposure to the kind of projects they tackled and how they engaged with clients. I continuously made sure I was learning but also that I was working well and internalizing what would be expected of me. I had set the bar high for myself ever since I was young, and I was finally learning from people who were in the roles I aspired to one day be in myself.

On many occasions, the audit teams would make sure to integrate my internship assignments with my college work. For instance, I would be given an area to audit based on my current school curriculum. I was not only assisted, but they also taught me all the right questions to ask the client while I was completing the internship assignment. I had the opportunity to accompany them when they were dealing with clients. I sat with them and did the real work they were doing. They helped ensure I was learning the college course work while at the same time experiencing how that work would play out in a real work environment.

Beyond the corporate work, the career development organization had a plethora of extracurricular learning opportunities it offered as well. We were highly encouraged to attend these events on Saturdays. The idea was that if we were able to make the commitment to ourselves to show up on Saturday after a hectic week of school and work, we would be rewarded by the extra skills we acquired. One important lesson I learned during this time was the benefit of going that extra mile, even if you feel like you have enough opportunities already. There should be no limit to the amount of preparation you are willing to endure. The more you work, the better the outcomes.

I also learned how many people thought it was ridiculous for me to be expected to attend events on the weekend after a full week of work and school. The question I encountered most frequently was "Why do you give up your personal time to go to these things?"

I always responded that I was not giving up my time; I was investing my time to acquire new skills. I was making a choice to spend my time on becoming a better version of me.

Many of the lessons were intellectual, some were behavioral, while others were experiential. I will always remember one event that taught me a valuable lesson, one I will never forget. There was a gala on a Saturday where we were required to dress appropriately for a business event. It was an evening event where our parents could come, and I was quite excited to attend it. I told my parents I needed to be dressed up for the event. I asked one of my friends what I should wear, and she recommended I buy a cute dress. We went shopping, and I chose a purple dress. My parents approved of it as well. All of us loved that dress, and to be fair, it was a beautiful one. It was my first-ever business gala, and I wanted to look my best. I most certainly didn't know I was supposed to be dressed in professional business attire. And so I went to the business gala in a purple dress. I felt out of place as soon as I entered the venue. Everyone was dressed like they were going to work.

During the evening, I felt so uncomfortable. I was not the only person who did not have a suit on, but I was one of the few who stood out in the room because we were the stars of the show. I was completely embarrassed, and I could see the others who hadn't understood the dress code were hanging their heads as well. Our good night felt anything other than good because we did not feel like we fit in. In the reception area before the gala started, our director made a comment to the broader group about our attire. My fears of not fitting in were confirmed when the director said, "Some of us are dressed like we are attending a Prince concert instead of a business gala." While he did not address me personally, I felt his comment was directly aimed at me.

He advised us we would have a session on corporate etiquette and dress codes to ensure we would always understand the significance of being dressed appropriately. The criticism was definitely constructive, albeit extremely direct, and I certainly appreciated the reality check. But at that moment, I was humiliated beyond all measure.

For weeks, I wondered why I didn't get that right. Certainly, there must have been something wrong with my judgment. I wondered how long I would last in the life I was signing up for, and if I even deserved it. I felt like Cinderella at that moment, except I refused to run out of the gala at the strike of trouble. I made the decision to attend it with grace and learn from my experience.

I have realized there are two ways you learn in life, and both of them are equally important. You learn from other people's experiences, by internalizing their core values and work ethic, and you learn by making mistakes and reforming yourself. I decided my learning was on the right track because I already had exposure to other people's experiences. I had been missing a mistake, and I had finally made it. I decided not to view a mistake in the negative light that most people view it in, and that has made all the difference for my self-image. I remember thinking, *Failures are opportunities to learn*. At that moment, I realized the significance of your personal brand and the need to preserve the reputation of others who have placed the value of their brand on you.

I learned two other valuable lessons that night, and both remain at the front of my mind today. Always make sure you know the dress code when attending an event. The other valuable lesson I learned was to be sure to seek guidance from someone who is qualified to give it to you. I had sought advice and counsel from someone who could not advise me on business matters.

That being said, it was certainly not easy coming to terms with the fact that perhaps other people got it right because they were surrounded by people who understood the realities of corporate and professional life better than my personal network did. It was rough not being able to find that level of support in my personal community, but that is what made me self-reliant, and that is a lesson everyone should learn, regardless of whether or not their community is capable of being supportive. I decided I would compare myself to others only if it allowed me to grow; I would stop comparing circumstances and factors I could not change, for that would do me no good.

That is another virtue the career development organization helped me polish because we were constantly urged to pay attention to what people around us in our internships were doing and how they were doing it. If we were unable to perform as well as those around us or were lacking in a certain area, we needed to increase our focus and change our approach. But we needed to excel. Of course, you should develop your unique approach to your professional life. But before you can do that, you need to interact with successful people in similar roles to understand the core dynamics that helped form the pathways to their achievements.

When I first started my internship, Christine M and Nancy M were my advisers. I worked with audit teams on their audit assignments. Sometimes I was able to travel with the teams and stay in really nice hotels during the workweek. These were the same kinds of business trips I had imagined people flying off to during my airport adventures with my father. It made me feel like I was finally making my childhood dreams come true. I would pause and reflect on those moments when I dreamed of the life I was actually living.

Early in my internship, I was able to help at the scheduling desk, checking in audit staff for their daily assignments. The technology was not what it is today, so every morning, the client groups had to call into the staffing desk to inform them where they were. Through this process, I got the opportunity to meet lots of people, because we would exchange pleasantries every morning. It also gave me the responsibility of accounting for our people, which I learned was a critical task. As an intern, I assumed it was just a task to keep me busy. I did not realize until later how significant that assignment was and how all the corporate client billing was based on those time reconciliations. I also did not understand the value of the casual connections I was making until later in my career. As an intern, I was able to experience a lot of things beyond the normal day-to-day work, which helped prepare me for my career after college.

I was able to participate in group projects. One was helping plan the company picnic, which was like a championship event where one team would win and have bragging rights for the year. There was a team of people at all levels, and I was allowed to work with them. This experience gave me the opportunity to meet people at all levels. I remember going shopping with one of the partners to buy items for the event. This shopping excursion gave us time to talk while doing something other than working. We talked about how we grew up, and we talked about school. He provided me guidance regarding college and career choices. He explained the types of audits I should look to be on and the people I should connect myself with. These conversations posed invaluable lessons, as I learned a considerable amount during this time together. I was learning who the top talent was, what the best assignments were, and how to make choices. I was also gaining an ally in the process.

While in college, I returned home each summer to work at my internship. I was also able to work during winter break to gain more experience. During the winter break of my sophomore year, I was asked why I went to school away from home. I was presented with the idea of transferring home to go to school. The idea was for me to go to school with a full-time course load and work a full-time schedule. There was an audit team working on a large client within walking distance from the local university that would create a role for me. That was a no-brainer. It meant I would be gaining hands-on practical knowledge while I was learning the course materials. The senior on the job, Greg, became not only my manager but my mentor as well. This was a perfect learning experience and was made possible because Greg was willing to put in the time to guide and coach me along the way.

I did not have anyone at home who understood what I was doing—or the struggles and challenges. They looked at me like I was a failure for transferring schools and coming home to go to a local university. To them, it was, "Kim left a good college so she could come home and work." In actuality, I had left a good school to go to another good school and have the invaluable experience of learning the course materials in a real-life environment while learning the textbook content. That was something my family didn't understand. After a while, I stopped trying to explain it. I stopped trying to defend my decisions. I knew one day it would all be clear and make sense to them. I knew my truth, and that was enough.

The team had several levels between the seniors and me. And everyone, from the new college graduates settling into their careers to the partners in the office, made me feel valued and comfortable. I didn't know what it was then, but I realize now that was the culture of the organization. It was the place that made me feel good about myself. In today's terms, I would say it was the place where I felt like I belonged.

As audit teams go, I was the lowest team member on the hierarchy because I had the least amount of experience. Heck, I didn't even have a college degree yet. So, the work I was doing was more administrative. But the team was always willing to teach. I recall having to go into this massive corporate office space, with a document in hand, to review bound copies of board documents and ensure the documents were the same. I recall thinking how ridiculous that seemed, and I thought they were just keeping me busy and out of their way. I learned later in my classes how significant that process was. There was a legitimate reason to do the work I was doing. Having that understanding made me feel like a valued part of the team. I made a lot of copies. A lot. A whole lot. And I faxed documents all the time—back when faxing was a thing. I remember being told I was allowed to read the documents because I was a member of the team and had signed a non-disclosure agreement. That taught me to remember to always look for the learning opportunity in any assignment I was given, no matter how tedious or mundane the task seemed to be. There is always something to learn.

This action proved important once when I went to fax something. I lifted the cover sheet and realized I had been given the wrong information. If I had not read it, we would have sent one client's information to another client. More and more, I felt like part of the team, and I was learning—though in an unorthodox manner.

I recall we were studying a chapter on the various inventory methods. When my senior learned of this, he sent me on a client inventory one weekend with an audit team. It was moments like that when I realized I was not just an intern; I was a part of the team. They made me feel welcomed. They trusted me to do a good job, and they taught me things to help me learn. More importantly, they made me feel comfortable when I didn't understand what I was doing or why I was doing it. It was OK to make a mistake. To use the wrong word. To reach for the wrong fork at a meal. To ask what "tartare" is when the raw meat showed up at the table. Confession—that was a learning moment for sure. I had never seen someone eat raw meat, and it was a bit unsettling. I honestly thought my stomach was going to erupt the moment I saw the red meat being consumed by others at the table. I didn't know how to respond when offered a piece. Part of me would have assumed it was rude to not try it. However, they had created an environment where it was comfortable for me to feel uncomfortable and ask any question I had on my mind. They all had experiences I didn't have, and that was OK. I learned it was OK to be different. They accepted me for who I was, and they wanted to create a path for me to become who I wanted to become. While they presented me with many first-time experiences, and I was open-minded and willing to try, I have to say the tartare was not something I was willing to experience. To this day, that has not changed.

Over the years, I worked and went to school. In my senior year, we were given an assignment that fell right in line with the work I was doing at my internship. This was my moment to shine. Greg and the team helped me think through my assignment and gave me time to get it done well. I aced the exercise, and while I was proud of myself, it felt good to know they were proud of me too. What I realized was that it was my space to grow and be challenged.

Chapter 12

KINDNESS OF STRANGERS

After graduating from college, I received several job offers. I had originally selected my internship because the people I met gave off the best vibes about the culture of the company. Having no real work experience, I needed to rely on my gut feelings to reach my decision. Too often in life, people do not tune into their bodies, not realizing that the mind and body are more in sync than they could fathom. A gut feeling is not something to take lightly because it is a quick assessment based on solid facts from your past experiences.

I realized I might not have had parents who understood the world I wanted to enter to a great degree, but I did know what love and support meant. I knew encouragement and kindness were virtues I was exposed to in the company of my father and brother and that those virtues built me up. I was not about to leave those virtues simply because I was entering professional life in what seemed like an entirely different world. I believe it was one of the best decisions I could have made; if I needed the semblance of familiarity in this new world, these virtues were the most fruitful to take along.

It is said that you are the company you keep. You certainly attract the kind of energy you put out into the world, and I strongly believe that if you are looking for something passionately enough, the universe aligns you with people who become enablers in your journey. It also ensures you find the resources you require to reach your desired goal. The bottom line is how badly you want to unlock your potential and the fate that you are destined for if you put in enough effort.

My transition from college into my first corporate role was seamless because my internship was a complete immersion into corporate life. Since I started my experience before even going to college, it was a perfect example of what I could expect after college.

I mentioned one of my advisers named Christine. Christine helped me transition into corporate life with unprecedented ease, despite everything being such a novel experience for me. Christine took a generous interest in my well-being and made a personal commitment to my development. I could not believe that someone would be genuinely interested in wanting to see me, a stranger, succeed. So many people from my neighborhood had either misunderstood me or shunned me, despite knowing me for years.

Meeting Christine made me realize that sometimes people you have just met are able to sense something in you (perhaps due to their experience and polished intuition) better than those you have been acquainted with your whole life. She redefined the term *family* for me, allowing me to consider it more inclusive than I ever thought I would. Although I must say, not everyone who fosters your growth becomes family. Sometimes people come into your life for a brief interval, and your exchange with them offers you a skill you need at that juncture in your life, or vice versa. Of course, you carry that skill with you, but that may be all that remains of your relationship with the person if that was their purpose in your life.

The significance of Greg in my life was huge; everything I did after working with him was because of everything he did to teach me while I was working with him. My professional relationship with Christine was similar. The personal part of the connection came as a complete surprise to me, and the significance of her in my life is something I will never forget.

Christine often dropped me off at home following my daily internship assignment so that I did not have to take a city bus late at night. I remember feeling embarrassed, not wanting her to find out where I lived. That was a foreign sentiment for me. I had never felt bad about where I lived, and I honestly never had anything to compare it with until I experienced the lives of others outside of my world. I tried to navigate why I was feeling that way and realized it was inevitable once I saw that people around me came from relatively well-off backgrounds that provided them with access and opportunity to the resources they needed. I often felt out of place, but they would quickly take those thoughts out of my mind.

One night, it was raining. Christine offered to drop me off at my front door rather than at the traffic light. I told her it wasn't necessary. I just had to run a few doors down the street, and I didn't want her to miss the traffic light. I always timed it perfectly. I would talk to her until the light was about to turn green. Then I would jump out of the car so she could make the traffic light. I normally walked slowly, allowing her time to cross the intersection and take the turn that led her out of the neighborhood. On this night, the rain was coming down really hard, and I was just trying not to get too wet. This time, I ran off, head down. As I was entering the door, I realized she didn't drive away; she missed the light and had to wait. She waved as she saw me opening the door to walk inside. I was mortified. *What should I do? Should I pretend I don't live here? In the apartments on top of the Stuffy's fried chicken restaurant on the corner of Springfield Avenue and Grove Street?* The moment was awkward. I hadn't been honest, but I had not been dishonest either. I had just found a comfortable situation where I didn't have to expose my urban living circumstances to someone who hadn't had to experience life on that level. That was a shame I could not manage. I did not want anyone to see the reality of my life. I was not sure at that point how my personal and professional lives intersected because I was trying to fit into a new environment. I was hoping to change the trajectory of my life. But at that moment, I felt exposed. I could not sleep all night.

The next morning, I was anxious about seeing her. I was afraid of what she would say, how she would feel, and if she would come to conclusions about me that were biased. I did not want her to feel bad for me or pity me; all I wanted was to be treated like everyone else. After school, I went to the office, and Christine was there. I had thought about all the possible things she could say to me overnight. But all she said was "From now on, I drop you off at the door. Deal?" I was overwhelmed. Instead of putting me down or creating obstructions for me, she accepted me. I was not used to unconditional acceptance of that nature, and it was a truly healing experience. "Deal," I said. And we never mentioned it again.

When the time came for me to get a place of my own, I was still in college. Christine provided the temporary financial support to ensure I could have a place with access to get to school and to work. She was my internship adviser, but more importantly, she was a caring human being who wanted to see me succeed. Her willingness to be the gateway to my path forward is something I will never forget.

My experiences with Christine and Greg taught me the significance of building a network of people who want to lift you up when you need a boost. They demonstrated the consistent uplifting support during my initial corporate experiences, which built the foundation for my future success. With them, I learned there was nothing embarrassing about grabbing on to a helping hand. Ironically, to become independent, you need to learn how to choose the right people to become dependent upon during the process. Independence does not mean cutting off ties but nurturing the right ones.

PART III

PURPOSE, PASSION, LEGACY

Chapter 13

DIFFERENT CAN BE GOOD

MY EXPERIENCES MADE ME GRATEFUL; they also made me realize that my path would have been considerably rockier had I not had the support of the people I encountered over the years. The realization inculcated within me a fervent aspiration to extend a helping hand toward those who are going through similar struggles. I made it my mission to talk to people about how being different could be conducive to growth and how societal norms do not always get it right. I would not be where I am today had people not seen in me things I could barely see in myself. No one deserves to live with a blurred vision of their capabilities, and everyone should be allowed to follow their dreams.

It took me time to realize that there was no harm

in letting my background define me. The fact of the matter was that I was different, and I slowly accepted that maybe it was not a bad thing. I was different because my path wasn't the same. I wasn't starting from the same place as those with generations of successful relatives. I had a cavernous gap of experiences and exposures to fill, and I would need to put in the extra work to close that gap. It only reasserted the fact that I had to work twice as hard to reach the same position as my coworkers. And I had to be OK with that, or I would have been stuck wallowing in pity.

I worked hard, and I learned a lot. And the people around me challenged me to do more and to do better. A couple of years into my audit career, it was time to take the CPA exam. This was something I knew I wanted to do as a way to differentiate myself in our field of study. I also knew it was a tough exam, with only a 50 percent passing rate. I had made some really good friends along my career journey and at work, and we were all in the same stage of our professional careers. We decided we would create a support system through the review courses and the preparation so we could feel more comfortable about the journey ahead of us. We studied to the best of our abilities. At the time, you had to take all four parts in the same sitting. It was all paper based, and you could not use a calculator. The minimum score to pass was seventy-five. You had to pass two parts to keep any passed parts. If you failed a part, you had to get at least a fifty to keep any parts. In short, the goal was to aim for a seventy-five in all the parts. If you passed all four, that would be ideal. If you landed with a few parts you could keep, that would be great. But you did not want to pass some parts and not have them count because you received less than a fifty on other parts.

There was a lot of material to cover, and I was used to spending multiple hours studying, but it was a big jump from the coursework I was used to. I did not pass all four parts during my first attempt. I was disheartened and disillusioned at first, and my worst fears about not being good enough came into play. But by that point, I was able to overcome them with a bit of encouragement from my friends. I had passed two parts and received a high enough score on the other parts to keep them. During the next attempt, I passed the other two. I could not believe I was officially a CPA. I was proud that I had accomplished another goal on my list of dreams, and I was beginning to feel less fearful. I was beginning to realize there was a possibility of actually achieving the things I had dreamed about.

No one in my family understood what the significance

of passing the CPA exam meant, and it made me sad that they did not know it was an achievement to celebrate. To them, it was just a test. My work colleagues, some who were becoming my close friends, understood and appreciated the accomplishment. That felt good to me, having someone around who could understand. I began to realize the importance of being surrounded by a supportive group of friends and colleagues with goals similar to mine. They were always around to cheer me on, to give me support, and to challenge me. This has been such a significant part of my growth.

Chapter 14

FOCUSED COMMITMENT

IN EACH ROLE I TOOK, I APPROACHED IT WITH THE notion of giving it all I had to give, making it better than I found it, and moving on to what was next. I had many great experiences and overcame many obstacles, the most important of which was realizing that I needed to feel like I was growing along with the role. I took advantage of the moment to advise my protégé that the moment it feels like you have outgrown your role, it is your duty to yourself to expand your horizons. Those who wish you success will support you in the transition to whatever is next.

After a few years at the accounting firm, I was passing a partner in the hall, and he asked me if I wanted to work on one of his clients. I was excited, and I leaped toward the opportunity. I passed the scheduling desk, which I was extremely familiar with, and I asked them to put me on his open client. They advised me he was looking to staff a heavy senior, someone about to make the turn to a manager. I was not even a first-year senior at that point; I would be one the following year.

When I went back to speak with him, he asked me how long I had been there. I realized at that moment that some people were so used to seeing me around, they thought I had more seniority than I actually had. It dawned on me that they liked me. For some of the staff members, I had been around since their first day on the job. I had helped them find their way around and helped with corporate politics. As an intern for four years, I had learned a lot. But now I needed to be evaluated and measured based on my performance, not based on how much they liked me. And this was a pivot I needed to make.

I decided I should change firms. It was a challenging decision to make. After having all of the assignments I wanted, all the access and exposure I could have dreamed of, after all they had done for me, I wanted to leave. I was in that same place I had once been in with my father, when having to choose a school and a career path. I was fearful of appearing ungrateful, anxious to see what else was out there. I talked it through with several people, and they understood. One of the partners asked me what I wanted to do. I told him I wanted to work on Wall Street. I had learned so much about the significance of the market, and I wanted to have a chance to be among the allure of the Financial District in Manhattan. They didn't hesitate to leverage their network to help me find my next opportunity. I embraced it as I had always done every other opportunity—with curiosity and a commitment to succeed.

Over the years, individuals in my network made connections and cleared paths to create opportunities for me. I was always grateful for their support and sponsorship. To maintain trust and never tarnish a referral, I remained committed to ensuring there would never be a situation when someone would regret endorsing me. My goal was to execute and deliver and always make it easy for someone to refer me going forward. This was a critical trait I leveraged during several subsequent career moves. When people believe in you and can count on you to demonstrate consistent performance, there is a comfort in endorsing you without fear of blemishing their brand. What I learned is that I needed to do the work to gain the trust and support before seeking mentorship and sponsorship.

Chapter 15

ASK FOR WHAT YOU WANT

As we shifted our discussion toward mentorship and sponsorship, a perfect example scenario came to mind, and I thought it would drive the message home for my protégé. Since we were being candid and transparent, I was suddenly very comfortable sharing a story I hadn't shared with many people about a pivotal moment in my career.

I recall asking an executive leader if I could be assigned to one of his upcoming projects. He responded by telling me he did not hire women to work on his client engagements because they cry and get pregnant. I thought he was joking at the time he said that to me. However, I looked at his project teams and realized there were only men—no women. At the time he said that, I did not think much of it. I had asked a direct question, and he had given me a direct, honest response.

In today's environment, it would be illegal to employ this type of talent-management process. Actually, it should have been illegal then, based on EEOC laws. I wasn't aware of that at the time, and he clearly wasn't concerned about the legality of his statement, because he made it so matter-of-factly to me. It was his policy, and the facts of his staffing data were in sync with his beliefs. However, I was not willing to simply take no for an answer. So, I challenged him to make an exception. At the time, I had become familiar with his competitive nature, based on our corporate team-engagement events. So, I decided to create an opportunity for him to prove he was right in a noncritical space. I was only asking for an entry-level role. There was little risk to the success of his engagement if he added me to the team.

The upside for me was having the opportunity to learn a different industry and to work with a highly rated team. Our agreement was this: he would never see me cry. That did not mean I would never cry. That just meant I would make sure any emotions I experienced, which resulted in tears, would be shielded from him. He agreed to that and reminded me that I could raise my voice. I could also cuss and pound my fists on the desk. All of these things were allowed, but crying was not. While it made no sense to me, he reminded me that in his world, the game was played by his rules. So, I agreed. Touché.

Now, for the pregnancy part, I explained to him I was single and focused on my career; pregnancy was not part of my plans. Therefore, he did not need to worry about that with me at this stage of my life. As we were having that conversation, I realized how uncomfortable the discussion was for both of us. However, the candid conversation was the catalyst that I needed to secure a position on the team. So, it was a discussion that needed to be had. And then we were done.

He agreed to give me a role in the assignment. The funny thing is that the timeline was only for a six-month term—less time than it takes for a woman's body to create a life. At that moment, I realized how trivial our entire discussion was—comparing the creation of life with the success of his audit. Although it seems like a trivial event, and a short-term assignment may not be perceived as being critical, this opportunity allowed me to expand my skills in the company of a top-rated, all white, all male team. It also demonstrated to others that hard work and tenacity could get me to the table and on a coveted assignment on the team.

More significant than my personal self-discovery is realization of the impact such beliefs have had on the careers of others who deserve a chance. Such thought processes limit opportunities for people who are in no way, shape, or form any less intellectually gifted than their counterparts. Not only that, but such thinking comes from the assumption that all women should want children. These generalizations present barriers for individuals who are looking for opportunities similar to their counterparts. Women have proven to be brilliant multitaskers. Their ability to run a household and manage a career demonstrates some of their superpowers. The thought that women would not be able to contribute to the success of a team if they choose motherhood places limits on the opportunities presented to them. If a man can be a father and a professional, why can't a woman?

As I look for the message to convey to my protégé, I pause to reflect on the point of our discussion. I was lucky enough to be surrounded by people who believed in creating opportunities for others. My journey allowed me to encounter people who didn't define me based on stereotypes. Most importantly, I was purposeful in charting my path because I was hardworking and focused. These are traits anyone can possess, if they are willing. The most important takeaway is to never accept no for an answer when you believe a yes is possible to obtain.

As we continued this conversation, we double-clicked on these thoughts, and I vividly recall a situation that required me to demonstrate my commitment to being a part of the team I had worked so diligently to earn a spot on. As I mentioned, I was the only woman on a team consisting of extremely talented men. Most of the guys knew one another from boarding school and from their civic engagements. They were not only colleagues and teammates; they were also friends. I, of course, was not from their communities, so I was not familiar with their civic relationships, and I was not part of their circle. I was just a teammate—an outsider who was trying to do my job. Many afternoons, I was the only one in our office space for long periods of time. Our workdays were extremely long, oftentimes crossing over into the late-evening hours. I often wondered where they would all disappear to in the late afternoons. Every time they returned, they would tell me they had been in a meeting. It seemed as if they were in meetings together for several hours in the afternoons and evenings.

One evening when they returned to the office, I asked one of the guys where they had been and asked if I could go with them the next time. He advised me it was a place I would not want to go. I found that to be odd. I was part of the team, working on the same deals. If they were having meetings about work, why wouldn't I want to go? I didn't push the issue but paid attention for the next few days. We were getting close to preparing pitch books for a deal road show, and I watched everyone get up to leave. This time I paid attention. I snuck a peek at the handwritten calendar on someone's desk and noticed there was a meeting scheduled in conference room P. I waited until everyone left, and I started asking coworkers from other teams if they could tell me where conference room P was. Several people said they had never heard of that room. Others tried to look on the scheduling system to help me locate which floor it was on, because it was not on the forty-second floor where we sat.

Finally, one person knew exactly where conference room P was. And he offered to take me because he was on his way to meet the team there. When we got to the elevator, he pushed the button for the lobby. I assumed we were switching to another elevator bank. Then we headed for the front door. That still didn't raise an eyebrow because we had several office buildings on the block. It was customary for us to move between buildings to meet with other teams during the day. What happened next did in fact raise my eyebrows.

We headed across the street and into a bar. I had been there many times before. But we didn't stop at the bar. We kept walking to a set of stairs. We descended the stairs and entered a gentleman's club. The entire team was there. So, this was where they would meet to think and talk and strategize. Now I understood why I had been told I wouldn't want to go with them. Since the team had always been comprised of men, their preferred meeting location was this place—close to the office but away from the office atmosphere. This was their thinking place. Apparently, this was a normal situation. The guys had not even considered how this was inappropriate now that a woman was part of the team. My curiosity drove me to figure out what was happening in those meetings, so I stayed. I had been given the opportunity to be on the team, so I had only one choice—to be a part of the team and sit comfortably in conference room P so I could be a part of the discussion.

Sometimes you have to do things you don't want to do in order to learn. My motto is this: if it is not immoral, unethical, or illegal … I will consider it. One may question the morality of conference room P, but in that moment, at that time, it was acceptable and was normal for the team. My desire to not be there was not going to cost me the learning opportunity I had longed for. My goal now was to get them to move the meetings to a place I was comfortable going. And I did exactly that after earning their trust and respect. It was a win-win all around.

I was not willing to remain uninformed just because the men at my firm had normalized certain domains as male dominated. I needed to actively change that narrative. At first, I began fitting in. But then I realized merely fitting in was not enough. I needed to learn to ask for what I wanted so that I would be heard. If I had not raised a concern, I would not have found a solution.

This reminded me of another experience, with an executive who was my manager during the midpoint of my career. I quickly learned his goal was to become the single leader of a group of products. At the time, he led two products in the group, but it was clear he had his sights on the entire space. The problem was there were already people leading the other products. One day during my one-on-one performance discussion, he asked me what my goal was on the team. My response was kind of melancholy: "I want to help you be successful." So, we had to work together to learn the spaces, build the business case to take them over, and establish a transition plan. In doing this work, we were able to consolidate all of the groups into one group, under his leadership, and streamline the functions to achieve cost savings. This was a significant win for the corporation, and it demonstrated the loyalty and commitment the team had. Having a great leader with a clear vision who believed in me and let me demonstrate what I could do in support of his goals was critical for my development.

Chapter 16
REFLECTIONS

SOMEWHERE ALONG THE JOURNEY, I STOPPED being afraid of asking questions. I stopped letting the biases define me. I realized I needed to find people who were where I wanted to be and ask them how they got there. Did they follow a strict routine? I realized I needed to set large and small goals and track my progress to keep me motivated. Even as I took small steps every day, I always made sure I was moving forward. I realized consistency is the key. I had to establish patience, set a timeline, and not allow myself to become discouraged if the pace was slow or if there were a few setbacks.

Positive affirmations kept me motivated during my journey. The more frequently I worked at my goals, the more energized and encouraged I became.

From the beginning, I kept pushing my limits until I redefined them.

With each accomplishment, large or small, it always felt liberating to act on my potential and to unlock people's minds from the biases they had associated with people like me. That being said, these biases formed a very real part of my experiences.

As I moved into jobs traditionally held by others, and moved up the career ladder into managerial or leadership roles, I often encountered resistance because I was not perceived as fitting the traditional, typical standard of success. This narrow view perpetuates a narrative that limits options and erects barriers to future career advancement for people like me.

To be able to persevere when the narrative is working against you requires resilience and an unbeatable desire to succeed. By the time I was a corporate executive, I had realized I needed a foolproof strategy to conquer my fears. This process contained many steps, and there were times when I felt like I was stepping back down instead of progressing. I kept practicing it until it became second nature to me.

First, I recognized where most of my fears came from—my childhood. Too often, people do not recognize the impact their upbringing can have on them. I implore upon you the significance of delving into your past for a successful future. If you faced criticism that you did not find constructive, that can be the foundation of insecurities and can have damaging results on your mindset. Often, you end up requiring constant reassurances. I was fortunate enough to find supportive people along the way who played that role for me, but I learned to reassure myself by trudging on even when things were the hardest. This resolve allowed me to respect myself more.

Perfectionism was also at the root of the fear of failure I had carried. I felt extreme bouts of pressure to perform well because there were so many eyes on me just because I had opted for a different route. Other than that, I often felt like I had to prove my decisions were right, and that took up the energy I could have used toward fulfilling my goals. Everyone will be convinced when you reap the results of what you sowed. Perfectionism born out of the fear of failure can be debilitating, such that you spend a lot of time contemplating whether you are the right fit for the job or if you should take a step or not. Even the remotest possibility of failure paralyzes you, and you spend time on the nitty-gritty instead of viable points toward progress. With time, I learned not to second-guess myself to the point of paralysis. Of course,

I still have days when I have doubts about myself. There are days when I carefully craft an email, then read it so many times to ensure it is well written. Those days, I remind myself that I am the only one who is truly aware of my fears and my limits, and because of that, I am the only one who can push past them.

Over the years, I saw that many people fail because of their ego-driven commitment to what worked in the past. I often saw this with people who felt comfortable and complacent in the current state, especially if they were the author of current-state practices. As new ideas were introduced, or current concepts were explored, they shy away from further innovation, afraid to let go of the past. Evolution is critical and significant. Someone once asked me, "Why take the risk of introducing change when we can hang on by doing nothing?" I decided I was always going to remain open to innovation because the world is dynamic. Someone I admired once said, "If you are not willing to change, you will have to accept the moment you become irrelevant, as everything will change around you." That resonated with me, and I have always remembered those words.

Everyone likes to succeed. The difficulty comes when fear of failure is the overriding emotion—when you can no longer accept the inevitability of making mistakes, or recognize the significance of trial and error in finding the best and most creative solution. The more innovative you are, the more slipups you are going to make. Get used to it. Determining to evade the errors will extinguish your creativity. Balance counts more than you think. Some tartness must season the sweetest dish. A little selfishness is valuable, even in the most considerate person. And a few letdowns are essential to preserving everyone's outlook regarding success. I learned to embrace the perplexities of life and revel in them.

We hear a lot about being positive. But we also need to appreciate that the negative parts of our lives and experience have just as indispensable a role to play in finding success, both in work and in life. Some crucial takeaways I have learned from the aforementioned experiences include the importance of continuously imagining what your ideal life looks like and what it means to you.

Who is standing by your side? How are you feeling? Are you happy and fulfilled? What does an ideal day look like? Most importantly, how do you intend to use your newfound status in society to help those around you struggling with their dreams? You are on a path of positivity and productivity, where you are in touch with your highest self, and an essential part of self-actualization is leading others to the same path of self-discovery. Moreover, if the dream is about more than yourself, it will allow you to expand your vision and realize that you are part of something much bigger than yourself.

Given the choice, I was not willing to sit back and let life happen to me. My preference was to figure out a way to orchestrate how my life would happen. I believed that everyone should have an opportunity to aim for improving their circumstances—if that was what they wanted—no matter where they came from. Life had a lot to offer to anyone who was willing to take a chance. To me, the risk was well worth the reward of seeing what I could accomplish and aiming for my dreams. I decided I wanted to give it a chance and try something different—do something unfamiliar.

Chapter 17

PURPOSE & PASSION

On my journey, I realized my true purpose and passion are helping others achieve their version of success. I have been extremely blessed to be in positions to provide career opportunities, guidance, and coaching for people. I have also been able to sponsor people into roles I thought would be good for them. Oftentimes, I have just been an ear and a safe space for someone to think out loud, with no fear of judgment. More importantly, I have been the person to provide encouragement and be the support someone needed when they felt the pressure to give up on their dreams.

Toward the end of my discussion with the protégé with big dreams, I decided to share some final thoughts and augment the discussion with stories and experiences.

One question my protégé sought clarity on was how a person can differentiate themselves during the hiring, selection, or promotion process. What is needed other than a great CV and a charming presence?

To respond to this, I leveraged information I gleaned when I asked one of my early career sponsors, Kristin, what she recalled to be the reason she hired me many years ago. She told me I was focused. I asked her to elaborate. Kristin advised me it was the look of desire and commitment in my eyes. She told me my gaze was alert and focused. She appreciated that I did not avoid any answers and did not seem to waver at any question. That confidence came from my desire to demonstrate I was worthy of the role. My prior experiences had taught me I would have to overcome the preconceived notions that entered the room with me before I ever had a chance to say hello—the stereotypes and generalizations related to the bias attached to my superficial, aesthetic being. There were also the embedded thoughts I had to overcome from my childhood, including the words "You better be smart." I needed to demonstrate I was capable. That was the source of my focus. We all know people who display empty bravado and hope others can't see through it. For me, it's about the confidence I exude, which is sourced in my courage to dream. That has become a fundamental aspect of my character. Another feature characteristic of my personality is my smile. Kristin let me know she immediately found my smile infectious and genuine. A lot of people might think that smiling will make them appear less confident and unsure of themselves, or too agreeable perhaps. Good energy is important to me, and I respond to it with a pleasant smile. That's my authentic self, and I am always genuine. Even when I am smiling, my enthusiasm is evident and doesn't undermine the fact that I am a force to be reckoned with. My determination and ambition are unprecedented and unparalleled.

All of these attributes are highlighting my successes, probably making it seem like I was always gifted and perceptive. But I am here to tell you that is not the case. I don't impress myself because I know there is always more growth to attain. I advise all of my protégés to avoid putting people on pedestals. In my opinion, the major differences between highly successful and average people are 1) the amount of hard work they are willing to put in, 2) how persistent they are, and 3) their readiness to evolve and unlock their potential.

It is only fair to couple this information with some interesting stories that highlight my evolution. These are tidbits Kristin remembered about me over the years:

"What I admire most about Kim is that she stays true to herself. When Kim arrived, her style was edgy and provocative for the time. So, when she walked into an old southern bank, I was anxious about how she'd be received. The trading floor, in particular, was full of arrogant men who wanted people to fit in.

"It was 2000, and the good ole boy club was in full glory. However, I knew Kim was capable, so I had to let go, allow her to do her job, and prepare myself for the blowback, as any good manager realizes. I sent her down to the trading floor in her stilettos. I waited. She came back happy and smiling. Later, I was told by the structured products exec to never send anyone but Kim.

"A few weeks later, a trading assistant said, 'Kim's smart, but you can't send her to the floor dressed so fashionably female like that.' I just laughed and said, 'We'll see.' I learned a lot from Kim, especially her sense of self and confidence.

"Kim was always put together. Her look—hair, nails, makeup, dress—was always important to her, and she *never* slacked off. One day after work, a group was going out for a beer a few blocks away. On her way, a mini tornado shot down the street. Those of us inside were standing on a bench to look out the window, watching people, newspaper stands, large branches, and Kim fly down the street.

"She was clinging to a light post for dear life, with her long, chiffon, maxi split cardigan swirling around her. Eventually, she made her way into the bar, with her hair standing straight up in the air and mascara running down her face. Always a good sport, she joined the group. She just laughed and laughed, ordered a drink, and enjoyed the moment.

"Kim and I had a boss who was a veritable genius but struggled to get the words out. He would provide explanations like "The equity. You know what I mean." One day, Kim plopped her butt on his desk and said, "No, I don't know what you mean, so I'm going to sit here until you finish the sentence." He fell in love with her spirit that day and vowed to sponsor her throughout her entire career."

As Kristin shared her memories, the one that hit me the hardest was this one:

"When she was a child growing up in the hood, even Kim's mom was unsupportive, but her dad and brother always believed in her. Kim got out of her situation because she had someone who believed in her. Many kids don't even have that, and without even one supporter, it's almost impossible to break the cycle."

The takeaway from this is knowing the balance between what the existing culture expects from you and what you can offer, knowing full well that it may be received hesitantly at first. But that is a good thing because it means you are going to be starting something new.

All successful people have at least one person in their lives who told them they could not make it. Imagine how many innovative methods and inventions would never have come into existence if they had given up. Do not ever be afraid to be yourself. The role may be defined beforehand, but once you step into it, it becomes a mold that takes your unique shape. So, just like you think about what your role has to offer you, spend time thinking about what you have to offer to your role.

As lunch was coming to an end, my protégé and I sipped the remaining contents of our water glasses and stood up for a long stretch. We had completed a deep, emotionally introspective discussion and were both energized and focused on our continued growth. We planned to meet at the same time in the same place for our next mentoring session. As we hugged, I noticed our hug was a bit tighter than I remembered from our prior meetings. Today was heavy, and our connection seemed to evolve as I opened more and shared more about my life. I looked to the sky as we walked away, and I smiled. There were so many things going through my mind. In that moment, I realized I should share my story.

Chapter 18

LEGACY & INTENT

THE MAIN INTENTION BEHIND WRITING THIS book was to share my story in the hope of helping someone who needs the courage to follow their dream. In my career, I have accomplished quite a few things people would define as successful. To me, everything has always been based on one thought: I wanted to escape the boundaries people expected of me. I wanted to follow my dreams and create opportunities for myself, knowing that, in the end, I would be able to create opportunities for others.

At one point in my career, I was part of an executive leadership program. One of the assignments was to write our legacy. I thought that was a strange and morbid assignment. I have never shared that with anyone before, but today I will share it with you.

When I think of legacy, I think of the people who have most impacted my life and how I remember them.

Growing up, my younger brother was a huge part of my life, and I remember him for the positive and loving impact he left on my heart and soul. He helped me believe that I could be better than I ever dreamed of. I was his hero (or shero, as he would call me) and I always wanted to make him proud. Because of him, I always wanted to do better and be better.

Many people who believed in me have given me opportunities that have helped me along my journey. Because of them, I have always felt the need to provide that same hope and assistance to others.

When I think of my legacy, I hope that my actions will help others to feel the same way my brother made me feel. I want people to remember me as a positive, no-nonsense, solutions-oriented, problem solver who isn't afraid to take risks. For people to remember me as a genuine, confident, strong, successful woman with a soft and giving heart.

While my life has had its fair share of obstacles and struggles, I want my life to shine a light on the fact that anyone with a dream, regardless of their socioeconomic or racial background, can truly achieve the success they seek. Beyond the professional success, I hope people will see, by my example, a woman who embraced all of life's experiences, whether up or down, with a smile and hopeful attitude. That on their individual journey, I can be an example to live a life full of experiences that bring both laughter and tears but ultimately bring true and complete fulfillment of dreams and goals.

While I hope the work I have done will speak for me in the end, I hope the manner in which I fearlessly embraced opportunities and challenges will resonate with others who have aspirations to fulfill their dreams.

We all need motivation and support. For me, one without the other doesn't work. I initially found both in my father and brother. But at the same time, I was surrounded by people who were not supportive and didn't pour into me with the energy I needed to face my fears. Instead, they fueled the fears and enhanced the insecurities. The consistency of the love, support, and motivation kept me grounded. Throughout my journey, I sought people, cultures, and environments where the energy was positive and the sponsorship was genuine. We have all had those people who are only willing to help you when there is something in it for them. Be wary of those types. Keep them close but not close enough to do harm. You are only valuable to them when they can benefit.

As I prepare to close my thoughts, I want to share the lessons I have described as I shared my journey with you:

1. Aim to be the best version of yourself.
2. Don't let other people's ideas limit your potential.
3. Be careful who you seek guidance from. If they haven't done it, they should not be telling you how to do it. Listen, but don't follow their lead.
4. Insecurities can cripple you or motivate you. You get to choose the impact.

5. Don't compare yourself to others. Be your unique, authentic self instead of mimicking someone else.
6. Find your safe space. Silence the noise and dream out loud.
7. Don't let your current situation define your scope.
8. Don't let people dim your light. People can only want for you what they can imagine for themselves.
9. Be comfortable moving forward. You may have to leave people behind as you follow your dreams.
10. It is impossible to live without failing, unless you live so cautiously that you are not enjoying the beauty of being alive.
11. We are all more vulnerable and a bit more sensitive than we are willing to admit to others, but we can't lie to ourselves.
12. You are responsible for your actions. Hold yourself accountable.
13. Imagine. Believe. Plan. Execute. In that order.
14. Be thankful.
15. Find a reason to celebrate you, and smile every day.

Chapter 19

TRUST BUT VERIFY

And as I always say, trust but verify. Up to this point, all of these words have been told to you by me—my version of my life. To hold myself accountable, I am sharing with you the stories of others. These are the unfiltered, unedited stories others have shared to describe how they have walked my path with me. I hope this helps you verify my messages and gives you the courage to dare to dream.

The following are some things people have said about me and the role I have played in their journey:

Jason

"I did not know I could be successful. It sounds crazy, but it is true. Kim is directly responsible for completely changing my worldview as it relates to my career in corporate America. Before I met Kim, I sat longingly on the sidelines, wishing I could be someone else. I was studying finance in college and had dreams of a career in corporate America. But I had no idea how to make this happen. I had no role models to follow, no positive examples, and no opportunities to pursue. All of this changed when I met Kim. I was blown away by her confidence, sense of purpose, and giving nature.

"I was not an easy case to work with. I was so self-doubting that even when presented the opportunity to apply for a job at a large global corporation, I was hesitant to try. Would I actually be enough? Kim knew something that I didn't, which is that the most important thing to do is to seize opportunities when they are presented, show up prepared, and be comfortable in one's own skin. Without her, I wouldn't have even started my journey, and all my potential would have been wasted.

"A few years into my role at the corporation, I was at another crossroads. I could either settle into my role as a financial analyst or attempt to accelerate my career by pursuing a top MBA. Kim encouraged me to not let up on my ambitions and go for the MBA. She provided much-needed support and guidance as I navigated the complex process of applying to a top-ten business school. That insidious sense of self-doubt I have crept up frequently, but now I had the tools to handle it. I persisted and earned my spot at the top-tier university.

"Since then, I've successfully competed for internships, full-time positions, and promotions. I've worked in strategic roles at top corporations and have developed the confidence I need to succeed. Every level of career advancement seems a little crazy in hindsight, but I've been able to rise to the occasion by assuming I belong, assuming I can perform, and assuming I am worthy. All of this can be traced back to me meeting Kim fifteen years ago."

Mouniratou

"I still remember the first time I met Kim at a conference. I was in awe by her personality, her charisma, and her attitude. She was what the kid will call these days 'goals.' I was too amazed to talk to her, so I just stared from far away. Later that year, she attended a meeting at our university. I was even more amazed that as a high-ranking executive at a corporation, she made time to attend a little meeting with a bunch of college students. I believe it was later on, as I kept seeing her at different functions, I finally found the courage to talk to her.

Since then, she has been an amazing addition to my life as a friend and mentor.

"I grew up around strong women in my life, but Kim brought a different strength and motivation to my life. I am a first-generation student, so many of my strong women role models barely finished school, while others never even attended school. From where she came to where she is today, she embodies perseverance, strength, beauty, and grace. In many ways, she has indirectly and directly established a path of possibilities for many people of color. She showed us that where you began in life does not define your future.

"Overall, I have learned numerous things from Kim, but one thing that sticks out to me is to dream and follow these dreams into fruition. Kim is a dreamer; she never stops dreaming and does not take anything for granted. In my opinion, this attitude is a key ingredient for success. She will recount the stories of her diverse adventures, whether abroad or at home, and I can see the excitement and joy it brought her. Through Kim's stories, I am able to dream bigger and am motivated to be the best self I can be. I am thankful for Kim and for guidance. She is truly an amazing individual and a blessing to our community and even the world."

Billy

"Courageous, boundless, energetic, inspiring, hardworking, confident, strategic, risk-taking, altruistic, and genuine.

"I met Kim during the summer of 2006. Kim was a senior leader and spearheading finance recruiting efforts for a global corporation at a conference in Fort Lauderdale. In typical Kim fashion, she was front and center at the recruiting booth and was the first person I saw walking into the venue. I was met with a dynamic personality. During our brief interaction, I told myself, 'I want to work for her!' She hired me. I began my career at the corporation. I was on her team for only a brief period, as she was quickly promoted to another role. Although my tenure on her team was short, Kim has had a profound impact on me personally and professionally.

"From day one, she took me in and treated me like family. She was like that big sister I never had. Kim has high expectations of not only her work peers but also of her friends. She sets the bar high and has a very low tolerance, if any, for mediocrity. If she believes you can do better, you will be made aware. While currently we live in different cities, she continually inspires from afar.

She often challenges those in her circle to do better by indirectly saying, 'I did this; I know you can too.'

"She pushes the envelope and sees no limit as to what she can achieve. She possesses a unique aura of confidence. When Kim puts her mind to do something, it gets done regardless of the obstacles encountered. She is a terrific leader—leading by example, encouraging, praising, and very candid with constructive feedback. She takes calculated risks and is very strategic in her approach. Most importantly, Kim is an even better friend."

Amanda

"Kim operates with integrity, hustle, and respect. She puts aside the social norms of the generation and focuses on the individual or task at hand. My first job out of college was at a bank where Kim was sitting in the C suite. I went to a Women in Finance meeting to try and get more involved, and I remember Kim walking up to me (in sparkly, high pumps) and introducing herself to me, as she did not recognize my face.

"She then began to ask me as many things as she could—where I was from, my educational background, hobbies, and my goals for the role I just accepted, including my career as a whole. She treated me respectfully and as her equal even though I was far below her and did not work on her team. She values your character, work ethic, and the way you treat others around you, and that is part of what makes her so special.

"The most influential thing that Kim has taught me is to understand my value, and she always makes me feel valued. She has shown me the importance of being your authentic self and having the courage to stand up for what you believe in. Kim is the living definition of the phrase 'Do no harm, but take no shit.' She is kind, genuine, passionate, charismatic, hardworking, and humble. She will respectfully speak up and challenge decisions that she does not agree with.

"She listens to understand and forms her own opinions; she does not let anyone influence her opinions, regardless of who it may be. What makes her different as a leader is that she consistently puts the greater good first and does not let her feelings, ego, or setbacks influence her decision. She has always made the decision she feels is best for the task at hand and encourages outside opinions to try and change her mind. There is no ego getting in the way of the work that she does, and I have yet to see that constant, humble work ethic with any other executive I have been fortunate to work with.

"As a friend and a mentor, Kim in the most supportive,

encouraging, and honest friend. She genuinely cares that I am my authentic self and stresses the importance of holding myself accountable and discipline. Her actions have taught me that no matter what situation I am in, if you are betting on yourself and willing to put in the work, you are not taking a risk.

"She has stressed the belief that any challenge that we may face is teaching us a lesson. That even though it may be hard, it is opening our eyes, and we should be grateful for the opportunity to grow and become a better version of ourselves—to believe in myself and the value that I bring to the table even, when I didn't even know what value I had.

"She puts my best interest as top priority and is always there to push me to be a better person because she believes in me. I have questioned her about why she takes the time to mentor and support me, and every time, she gives me the same answer, 'I am a leader. It is my responsibility to lift as I climb.' Whether it is in my personal life or career, when I am in a tough spot or need some guidance, I always ask myself what Kim would do in this situation. When I am unsure of what she would do, I just pick up the phone, and she is always there.

"To put it simply, Kim is the most inspirational individual there is, and I am blessed to know her."

Sacha

"Kim gave me my first opportunity in corporate America, and I am forever thankful to her for changing the trajectory of my life. Kim volunteered to take an active role in recruiting for a corporate rotational program, and through her leadership and selflessness, she singlehandedly increased the minority representation in the program. In fact, all my friends during my four years at that organization were hired directly or indirectly by Kim. In addition, Kim headed the Council for Diversity and Inclusion, another volunteer role, whereby she worked to educate colleagues on the value of hiring diverse talent. Kim got me a role on that council, which helped elevate my profile at the organization and in the program. Kim has served as a professional reference for me throughout my career. She wrote my recommendation for grad school (NYU Stern) and agreed to be my reference on two separate occasions for job opportunities, both of which I got. Kim has always been available when I call her to ask for career advice or to simply give her an update on my life.

"Beyond hiring me and providing references, Kim has sincerely been my professional role model. When I first started in the program, I didn't know how to succeed in corporate America. I lacked self-confidence, and I couldn't shake an overwhelming feeling that I didn't belong. Kim taught me that confidence comes from knowledge and that it is crucial to always be overprepared. She taught me to be myself and to never compromise my values or integrity. Witnessing the respect that Kim garnered from senior management at the company was impressive and still motivates me to strive for excellence. I am blessed to have Kim as a friend and mentor."

Diana

"Where to even start … I think the best way to sum it up is to say that you *saw* me and allowed me to see the authentic you. You being you gave me the courage to stand boldly, see myself, and bring my real self every single day.

"From our first conversation, I knew you were unlike anyone else I'd ever met and *definitely* unlike anyone I'd ever met in banking. Bold, honest, smart, stylish, and your real NY self. You've given me so many nuggets of unfiltered truth and wisdom that have stuck with me since my first interview with you.

"I watched you navigate finance, technology … bank politics and everything in between, all while not losing yourself. Before meeting you, I didn't believe it was possible to achieve success in banking in a way that still allowed me to be me. You showed me that was possible.

"On top of all of that, what's really transcendent for me is that not only were you able to serve as a role model simply by existing, you really, truly advocated for me. You pushed me to do more, to meet more people, to be better, all while speaking for me in rooms I was not in. And I cannot even count the number of times you have let me join you in rooms that I had no business being in at the time. I owe what I was able to do since meeting you to you.

"You inspire me in so many ways, but most of all, you inspire me to just *go for it*. There's no job too hard, vacation too crazy to take, and no outfit too fabulous to wear. I think your story will show people that if you are willing to put in the work … you can be yourself, uplift others, and *win*."

Maria

"Kim, I have been reflecting hard and long about the *huge* impact you've had on my life and probably many women of color in our industry. *You cannot be what you cannot see.*

"The first thing that comes to mind is *courage*. The

courage to be *bold*, *ambitious*, and *unapologetic* about your goals and dreams. I learned from you never to hide, minimize, or apologize for *who I am* and *who I want to be*. You lead by example because I watched you and followed your story through the years. I see you take bold opportunities, and you have remained yourself—wiser, *yes*, but still you.

"Traditionally, women are expected to hide, to adjust, to compromise. With you, there is none of that. You instead change the game altogether to fit you. You focus on performance—outcomes—and use that as leverage to influence a more inclusive environment for everyone. You, my dear, are a *creator* of reality. The second thing that comes to mind is *focus*. I learned from you never to be half-in or half-out. Commit 100 percent to the goal, give yourself in, and *focus* your energy into that dream. Nothing is worse than diluted energy. You lead by example. For the things you are passionate about, you do not see a job; you see a dream, you see opportunity, and you enjoy diving deep into what drives you. I also think of *innovative* and *groundbreaking*. You are not afraid to be first and be the first mover. You are comfortable being uncomfortable, and it is a great trait to have when you are trying to accomplish great things. You've had to be creative in a world with a lot of rules—rules you don't follow. *You make your own*, and we all benefit from it.

"Finally, I learned being *practical/flexible* from you. If it does not work, do not force it; let it go. You have made significant career moves. All have come with a practical and flexible mindset. You are good at adjusting your sails while keeping your goal in mind. You are a mother of many successful stories, including mine, and I am doing my best to live up to your legacy. I do hope to follow your steps and become as influential as you. *Love you to pieces!*"

Printed in the United States
by Baker & Taylor Publisher Services